Getting Your Community Coalition "Fired Up" for Change

Frances Dunn Butterfoss, PhD

Foreword by
Meredith Minkler, DrPH

authorHOUSE®

AuthorHouse™
1663 Liberty Drive
Bloomington, IN 47403
www.authorhouse.com
Phone: 1-800-839-8640

This book is a work of non-fiction. Names and places have been changed to protect the privacy of all individuals. The events and situations are true.

Published by AuthorHouse 05/14/2015

ISBN: 978-1-4918-1013-2 (sc)
ISBN: 978-1-4918-1012-5 (hc)
ISBN: 978-1-4918-1011-8 (e)

Library of Congress Control Number: 2013914775

Print information available on the last page.

This book is printed on acid-free paper.

For community builders everywhere whose dedication and passion ignite my heart and soul to do this work!

TABLE OF CONTENTS

Part I
Before You Build It!

Part II
Build It!

Part III
Make It Work!

Part IV
Sustain It!

Figures

Coalition Tools

"Coalition building" and "partnerships" have become buzz words for those seeking to make change in health, education, the environment, and other critical arenas in the early twenty-first century. With few exceptions, however, the books available for learning the whys, hows, and dos and don'ts of building and sustaining successful coalitions are largely oriented toward practitioners, academics, and others who participate in this work from the outside.

Internationally known coalition builder, writer, and scholar Fran Butterfoss helps fill this gap with this lively, easy-to-read, and exceedingly helpful book for those "in the trenches"—the neighborhood organizers, community builders, and others who are often the heart and soul of effective coalition building. This concise and accessible book also will delight students, professionals, and anyone who seeks a painless yet comprehensive understanding of coalitions and related collaborative partnerships.

An inveterate camper and outdoors person, Dr. Butterfoss keeps the fire-building analogy alive throughout this entertaining book as we learn about the kindling—or resources—needed to start the fire, the factors that come into play in sustenance and sustainability, and the need for conscious decision making about whether to "douse the fire" or keep it going with sound purpose and agenda. Using that imagery of the fire with concrete examples to keep the subject grounded in reality, Fran walks us through the process of creating coalitions and partnerships that last. She provides a wealth of check lists, tip sheets, websites, and other tools that can be used by coalitions wishing to assess their progress, look candidly at how they measure up on inclusiveness, and use "SWOT analyses" and other tools as they plan strategically to move ahead.

But, as Dr. Butterfoss herself points out, "Coalitions are never easy, [and] challenges arise every day when you combine the ideas, talents, and resources of diverse community sectors, coalitions, organizations, and individuals to reach effective actions." The book therefore asks hard questions and provides the tools we need to answer them—including those at the front end of the process: Is our group really a coalition? And is the coalition model the best to use given our goals and resources? If the answers are yes and our fire continues to flourish and grow, Fran provides simple guidelines for developing memorandums of understanding (MOUs), bylaws, and the like to take the mystery out of these aspects of the work, which is so essential for coalition success and staying power. Finally, *Ignite!* includes the simplest, most helpful approach to evaluation I've ever seen. In these ways alone, the book pays for itself as an invaluable "go-to" resource.

A skeptic once called coalitions and partnerships "unnatural acts between unconsenting adults." And when created solely to help fulfill a grant mandate or otherwise access needed resources, such skepticism may be justified. Yet, as Dr. Butterfoss clearly demonstrates, a coalition that is done well and for the right reasons can be a highly effective—and fun—way for a community and its partners to get "fired up for change." This book will help "light your fire," as it has mine.

Meredith Minkler, DrPH
Professor and Director, Health and Social Behavior
School of Public Health
University of California at Berkeley

PREFACE

We all share a primal link with fire. For the ancients, fire provided warmth, protection from wild animals, light in the dark wilderness, and heat to cook food. While fire is no longer the center of our existence, it still has a magnetic power that attracts us. The dancing flames of fire can inspire romance and legendary stories, generate uplifting discussion, and build camaraderie among those circled around them. And camping just isn't camping without a campfire ... the smell, the warmth, the crackle, the glowing coals, the smoky taste of campfire-cooked meals, the songs and stories, and, of course, the s' mores. Campfires provide a deep connection with nature, time for reflection, and feelings of peace.

As I was gathering wood for a campfire in the Shenandoah Mountains of Virginia last fall, I began to conjure up images of how much constructing and feeding one was like building and sustaining a community coalition. Coalitions have the power to catalyze a spark of an idea about how our communities could be healthier. This spark is fed by the imagination and resources of diverse community members and organizations working in partnership until we "fire up" entire sectors of our community for positive change. That's how an idea for a book often comes ... sudden and unbidden ... a flint-like notion that sparks a whole new thought process. So, as you read this book, keep the campfire analogy in the forefront of your conscious thought!

The following resources provided practical knowledge about building a campfire the right way!

- Campfire Dude. *Campfire Lays.* http://www.campfiredude.com/campfire-lays.html
- Essortment. *Learn How to Build a Campfire in Six Easy Steps.* http://www.essortment.com/build-campfire-6-steps-31318.html
- Love the Outdoors: Camping Tips and Outdoor Guides. How to Build a Campfire. http://www.lovetheoutdoors.com/camping/how_to_build_a_campfire.htm
- Smokey the Bear. *Campfire Safety.* http://www.smokeybear.com/campfire-safety.asp
- The Art of Manliness. *How to Build a Roaring Campfire.* http://artofmanliness.com/2008/09/04/how-to-build-a-roaring-campfire/

My textbook, *Coalitions and Partnerships in Community Health* (Jossey-Bass 2007), is a comprehensive, one-stop shop for coalition building that includes many tools and examples. However, its sheer length and breadth can be overwhelming for community builders and activists who are ready to do this work now. This shorter, more user-friendly book is created with them in mind. Please note that the terms "coalitions" and "partnerships" are used interchangeably in *Ignite*. While differences exist between them ("What Is a Coalition?" in part I), in practice, they often are used interchangeably, and I will make points that apply to either or both.

The following overview of stages will guide you through the organization of *Ignite*; it shows how the stages of building a campfire and a coalition are related to one another and divides the set of tasks into the four parts of the book: Before You Build It, Build It, Make It Work and Sustain It. This book can be read in any order. If you are a novice community builder, start at the beginning of part I and digest that information before moving on to parts II and III. If you are an experienced coalition builder, start at whatever stage or part you need to learn more about now. Coalitions may skip stages of development and revisit them when problems or needs arise. In other words, you can always read the other chapters later.

I wish you all the best in the vital work you do to build strong partnerships that change communities.

Part/Stage	Campfire	Coalition/Partnership
Part I Before You Build It	• Make sure the conditions are right (humidity, wind) • Decide on the kind and purpose of the fire (size; for warmth or recreation)	• Conduct an environmental scan or assessment (community readiness) • Decide on the purpose and kind of collaboration (formal/informal, size, for networking or action)
Part II Build It	• Gather the right kindling and wood • Build a good base or infrastructure • Decide who will keep the fire going	• Gather the right people • Build a structure for success (mission, roles, work groups, bylaws) • Choose and develop leadership
Part III Make It Work	• Start the fire (spark, match, lighter fluid?) • Find a ready supply of fuel	• Engage people in assessment and creating an action plan • Motivate and encourage to commit, participate, and share resources • Initiate strategies
Part IV Sustain It	• Build a good base of coals • Feed the fire when needed • Prepare for ebbing flames • Rebuild the fire or prepare to douse it when finished	• Identify financial and in-kind support to maintain strategies long enough to achieve outcomes • Sustain interest and energy in the work • Spin off strategies and change structure or processes if needed • Expand or end the collaboration when goals are reached

PART I
Before You Build It!

Before you ever strike a match, you are responsible for pre-fire planning. Whether you are making a fire for fun, cooking, or warmth, good decisions will ensure a safe and appropriate fire.

Decide whether you should build a campfire or not. There are fire-burning restrictions for every national park, state or federal forest, and all public land. Restrictions may range from "any fire any place" to "no fires at all," depending on fire danger levels and environmental impact issues. Campfires can become wildfires that destroy thousands of acres of wilderness and nearby homes when people make poor choices and build fires in high winds or low humidity. Only start a fire when conditions are favorable.

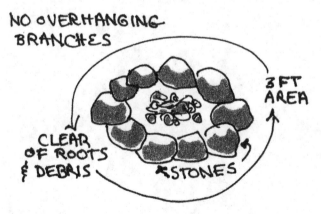

Choose your fire site. Once you decide to have a campfire, *where you actually build your fire* and *how you prepare the site* are critical. Your goal should be to leave *no trace of fire* once you move on, so minimize your impact by heeding the following tips:

- **Gather fuel.** Gather wood far away from camp and take only dead, downed branches.
- **Fire site.** Make a small fire that can be easily erased. If a fire ring is available, use it or build your own.
- **Disperse ashes.** Burn all wood down to ash and take it with you when you leave. Disperse it well off the trail, or you will attract others to overuse the same spot.

BEFORE YOU BUILD YOUR COALITION!

Before you decide to build a coalition, you must understand what this organization is and whether you actually need to build one to accomplish your community's work. Coalitions are complex entities that require significant investments of time and resources to establish and maintain. A general rule of thumb is not to build a coalition or partnership *if a simpler structure will get the job done or if the community does not embrace this approach.*

Why Collaborate?

Collaboration is at the root of all community building. Generally, collaboration occurs whenever people work together to achieve a common goal or goals. The kind of collaboration that is required of a coalition or partnership involves shared resources, rewards, responsibility, and risks, as well as mutual accountability for success (Mattesich and Monsey 2001, 7). This formal, sustained commitment allows organizations to achieve results that they would be less likely to achieve alone (Winer and Ray 1994, 24). Despite the rewards, organizations involved in collaborative efforts must understand and respect each other's self-interests (i.e., structure, agenda, values, and culture), relationships, linkages, and how power is shared and distributed (Gray 1996, 59).

Collaboration changes the way organizations work together. It moves organizations from competing to building consensus; from working alone to including others from diverse cultures, fields, and settings; from thinking mostly about activities, services, and programs to looking for complex, integrated interventions; and from focusing on short-term accomplishments to broad, systems changes (Winer and Ray 1994, 24).

Collective Impact

Collaboration is recognized as an essential ingredient of community building, although a new take on community collaboration is gaining attention across the country. The Strive Group tackled the student achievement crisis to improve graduation rates, reading and math scores, and preschool readiness in Cincinnati and northern Kentucky; the Elizabeth River Project engaged stakeholders over fifteen years to develop an eighteen-point plan to conserve more than 1,000 acres of the southeastern Virginia watershed by restoring water quality and wildlife that had been polluted by industrial waste; and Shape up Somerville involved the Massachusetts city to collectively define wellness and implement weight-gain-prevention practices in schools, restaurants, farmers' markets, businesses, and along walking routes to significantly decrease the body mass index among elementary school children between 2002 and 2005 (Kania and Kramer 2011, 38). The success of these initiatives is based on an approach called *collective impact,* the commitment of a group of actors from different sectors to a common agenda for solving a complex social problem.

Collective impact is more rigorous and specific than collaboration among organizations due to five conditions that lead to meaningful results (Kania and Kramer 2011, 39–40):

1. **Common agenda.** Participants have a shared vision for change, which includes a common understanding of the issue(s) and a joint approach to solving it through agreed-upon actions.
2. **Shared measurement.** Collecting data and measuring results consistently across all participants ensures that efforts remain aligned and participants hold each other accountable.
3. **Mutually reinforcing activities.** Participant activities are differentiated and coordinated through a mutually reinforcing action plan.
4. **Continuous communication.** Consistent, open communication is needed among players to build trust, assure mutual objectives, and appreciate common motivations.
5. **Backbone organization.** A separate organization with staff members who are skilled in facilitation and project/data manage-

ment serves as the backbone for the initiative and coordinates participating organizations. Backbone organizations focus people's attention and create a sense of urgency, apply pressure to stakeholders without overwhelming them, frame issues in a way that presents opportunities as well as difficulties, and mediate conflict among stakeholders (Kania and Kramer 2011, 40).

Ultimately, an effective coalition embodies the first four conditions of collective impact. The "backbone organization" may either be the coalition itself (if it is a non-profit organization) or the lead agency that convenes and supports the coalition.

What Is a Coalition?

In William Shakespeare's *Romeo and Juliet* (1600), he penned: "What's in a name? That which we call a rose, by any other name would smell as sweet." Similarly, we use many terms interchangeably to describe collaborations with mutual goals, even though each of these working relationships is different. Strictly speaking, a **coalition** is group of diverse organizations and constituencies working together toward a common goal (Feighery and Rodgers 1989, 1).

In this book, we will be concerned with community-level coalitions that operate in rural, urban, and suburban locations. A community coalition 1) serves a defined community recognized by those within it as a community (a common location or experience), but also serves the broader community; 2) is viewed by community residents as representing and serving them; and 3) reflects the community's diversity, both at grassroots and grasstops (professional) levels (Butterfoss et al. 1993, 316; Clarke et al. 2006, 15S).

Unlike networks whose member organizations act independently, coalitions bring organizations together to act jointly. Coalitions may form to address a specific, time-limited issue or may establish a more sustained collaboration (Chavis and Florin 1990, 20). They can help achieve population-level policy changes by focusing on multiple strategies with sufficient scale and scope. With a comprehensive action plan, a coalition can engage people, ideas, and resources across sectors and settings to create a synergy of health and prevention efforts that will have a lasting effect on people's health. Coalitions develop an internal decision-making and leadership structure that enables member organizations to speak with a united voice and engaged in shared planning and action. Links to outside organizations and communication channels are formal. Member organizations are willing to pull resources from their organizations, as well as seek new resources to develop a joint budget. Agreements, roles, benchmarks, and assignments are usually written.

A **partnership** is similarly defined; however, it often refers to a more business-like arrangement and may involve only two organizations or many more. Other collaborative relationships are defined as follows (Winer and Ray 1994, 23):

- **Network**—a loose-knit, non-hierarchical group of individuals and organizations with flexible roles, leadership and decision making.
- **Advisory committee**—a group that is formed at the request of an organization or person of authority (e.g., mayor) to provide review, advice or services, recommendations, and ideas. The group exists for input into decision making, not decision making itself, and is made up of professionals or citizens who represent different sectors of the community.
- **Commission**—a group that is appointed by an official body and is authorized to perform specific duties or steps or take on certain powers.
- **Federation, consortium, alliance, or league**—a union or connection of interests that have similar character, structure, or outlook; a semiofficial organization of organizations. Usually a central body of facilitative leaders develops semiformal links and a joint budget, and seeks new resources to coordinate tasks and limit duplication of services.
- **Executive board or committee**—a formal group that holds delegated power in a particular area and performs planning and governing functions for a larger collective body or organization. Participants are elected or appointed and represent specific organizations, sectors, or shareholders.

- **Task force**—a self-contained group of "doers" that is not ongoing. It is convened for a narrow purpose over a defined timeframe at the request of another body or committee.

The name of the organization is not as important as the fact that everyone agrees on its structure and purpose. However, if it is composed solely of individuals and not groups, then it is probably an organization or network and not a true coalition (Butterfoss 2007, 71). Coalitions operate at many levels—block, neighborhood, city, town, county, regional, state, national, international—and their scope, structure, and function will vary accordingly.

Why Do Coalitions Form?

Community coalitions often form in response to an opportunity, such as the release of the federal "stimulus funds" to promote healthy communities in 2009. They also may form because of a threat such as a national story about the rising prevalence of autism or a local outbreak of measles on a college campus. Local organizations may voluntarily form or join coalitions to augment their limited resources. Joining with other agencies and individuals can reduce duplication, maximize efficiency, and give organizations expanded access to media coverage, marketing services, community residents, influential community and professional networks, and expertise (Whitt 1993, 11). Coalitions also may be required by funders, such as the National Business Coalitions on Health community seed grant program.

Why Do Coalitions Work?

Coalitions provide four main benefits to those communities that choose to build them:

1. **Strength in numbers.** A main advantage of working in partnership is having the support, encouragement, and sheer numbers behind your effort. While one organization is composed of a given number of members, a coalition is composed of organizations, which multiplies the number of members available to carry out a strategy or support an advocacy action in exponential

fashion. Your mayor, state legislator, or school superintendent is more likely to work with your coalition because of the influence and representativeness of your membership.

2. **Strength in relationships.** Coalition building is all about relationship building. Organizations are invited to join a coalition because of their credibility, reputation, expertise, or resources. In cultivating strong relationships among your members, you will overcome obstacles and be more likely to reach mutual goals.

3. **Strength in diversity.** The knowledge and wisdom needed to solve the health or social issue of interest rests with community stakeholders who have direct experience in dealing with it. A strong coalition represents the breadth of the community in all of its unique diversity. When the experience of a coalition reaches across races, ethnicities, ages, special populations, education, income levels, and career paths, all perspectives will be represented fairly and fully. Your coalition will be able to view issues in all their complexity and develop solutions that are acceptable and more likely to work.

4. **Strength in resources.** Individuals and organizations bring tangible resources that will sustain your coalition and its efforts over the long haul. Resources may take the form of actual funds, expertise, influence, and connections to others. In-kind resources, such as meeting space, assistance with communications and technology, refreshments, or incentive items will help to engage your community in the work.

Assess Your Community

According to the campfire analogy at the beginning of this chapter, you should know the fire safety rules and regulations, do an environmental scan of the proposed site for risk factors, and either postpone your campfire building or prepare your site accordingly. Similarly, before you decide to build a coalition, you should do an environmental scan or assess the community that your coalition will serve. Each coalition is a unique product of the community it serves. Coalitions must be dynamic and responsive to cultural, racial, and ethnic diversity, and how people work together. Many of the following contextual factors within communities can influence and shape coalition development (Butterfoss and Kegler 2009, 254):

- Connectedness or linkages between individuals groups and organizations
- Political climate or history surrounding collaboration, power, and decision making
- Policies, laws, and regulations
- Environmental, in-kind, financial, and human resources
- Community motivation, readiness, and awareness of key issues
- Flexibility and adaptability in problem solving and task accomplishment
- Trust and ability to communicate to reach consensus among community sectors
- Existing identifiable leadership

Conducting a SWOT Analysis

Identifying these factors can be one part of doing a simple SWOT analysis with a group of knowledgeable community members in 60-90 minutes. SWOT elements are defined and illustrated in the following list and illustration:

- **Strengths**—internal factors that allow the coalition to take advantage of opportunities or reduce barriers
- **Weaknesses**—internal factors or challenges that prevent the coalition from taking advantage of opportunities or reducing barriers
- **Opportunities**—external factors that allow the coalition to take action, build membership, or improve the community
- **Threats**—external factors that hinder goal attainment, momentum, or long-term survival

Conducting a SWOT Analysis

	Helpful to achieving goals	Harmful to achieving goals
Internal coalition traits	Strengths	Weaknesses
External environmental traits	Opportunities	Threats

This process will help you to identify the community's assets and needs; specifically those of current and potential populations that you'll try to reach. The SWOT analysis process includes: 1) reviewing the strengths and weaknesses of your existing coalition (or potential organizations if you haven't built into a coalition yet); 2) reflecting on the community and broader environment in which your coalition (or its organizations) operates to identify the opportunities and threats that it faces; and 3) specifying *strategic issues* that your coalition should address and setting priorities in terms of time or importance.

Is a Coalition Right for Your Community Work?

After completing the SWOT analysis, another critical part of your community assessment is to decide whether to form a coalition or not. If you have many negative responses to the items in **TOOL 1: Is a Coalition Right for You?** you might consider building a limited partnership with one or two key community groups.

Decide on the kind and purpose of your collaboration. Now that you have reviewed the various kinds of collaborative relationships and completed your SWOT analysis, you probably have decided that collaboration is in the best interests of your community, you must decide what kind of collaborative working arrangement you will build. Since you are reading this book, I assume that you want to build a coalition or partnership. Being able to distinguish between different kinds of collaborative structures is critical, so that you will be able to take advantage of their strengths and purposes when you recruit organizations to join one. As for optimal size of the collaboration or coalition, membership may vary from a few to a few hundred individuals and organizations. The best idea is to start with a core group of key organizations, then recruit more members as you expand the scope and depth of your strategic initiatives. Don't worry about your coalition growing too large; you can always create working groups that make the work manageable.

Determine the general nature of your work. Will the coalition be convened primarily to share information and resources and reduce duplication of services? Will it be primarily an education and awareness building organization? Will you advocate for policy, systems and environmental (PSE) changes in your community? Coalitions that are more action oriented and strategic are more effective in reaching their missions and outcomes, as shown in **TOOL 1: Is a Coalition Right for You?**

TOOL 1: Is a Coalition Right for You?	YES	NO
1. Does the issue affect a broad range of people?	☐	☐
2. Is issue complex, requiring information and expertise from various sectors of the community?	☐	☐
3. Is broad public awareness or education needed?	☐	☐
4. Does a gap in services or programs exist, whereby no existing group is mandated to take on this work?	☐	☐
5. Do other organizations see this issue as a priority?	☐	☐
6. Are organizations willing to work together on the issue?	☐	☐
7. Is this issue best addressed through joint ownership and responsibility of a number of organizations?	☐	☐
8. Are potential members willing to relinquish control over coalition activities and outcomes to collaborate?	☐	☐
9. Are potential members willing to commit to and abide by democratic decision-making procedures?	☐	☐
10. Do organizational goals and policies of potential members align with those of the coalition?	☐	☐
11. Can resources be shared or obtained to do the work?	☐	☐
12. Are potential members committed to work together irrespective of funding commitments?	☐	☐
Ontario Healthy Communities Coalition 2002		

Programs and Events versus Policy, Systems, and Environmental (PSE) Change

Setting	Program/Event	PSE Change
School	Celebrate national Red Ribbon Week	Add alcohol abuse prevention to county high school curriculum
Community	Host community bike ride and parade	Implement policy to ensure that youth DUI laws are established and enforced in county
Worksite	Hold staff health screenings	Implement policy that offers workplace counseling for addictive behaviors
Local Business	Provide incentives for youth rally	Convene Business Council to set reasonable limits on retail distribution of alcohol, operating alcohol outlets and managing events where alcohol is sold

What about Competing Coalitions? Your community assessment also will identify assets, such as organizations and efforts that are already working on your issue or one that is related. What if your new coalition decides to deal with issues that already are the focus of another coalition or community group? You may have been unaware of the existing coalition or you may feel that the existing coalition is ineffective. In any case, your coalition may be seen as trying to duplicate, replace, or preempt other collaborative efforts, so try one of these options (Sofaer 2001, 10):

- Support and join the existing coalition, rather than starting a new one (review the following "Is this Group Really a Coalition?" tool to determine if the existing group is a coalition).
- Create a specialized coalition under the umbrella of the existing one.
- Start a new coalition anyway and coordinate efforts as much as possible.

- Network to build new individual and organizational relationships. Consider collaborating on a single event or short-term project to build trust and future work.

Sometimes, you may be asked to join or reform an existing coalition. You may be surprised to find that it does not fit your idea of what a coalition is supposed to look like or actually accomplish. Here, it might be helpful to use the following tool to assess whether it is a functioning coalition. Use **TOOL 2: Is This Group Really A Coalition?** to analyze your group.

TOOL 2: Is This Group Really A Coalition?

❑ The group is formed to address a specific, external issue.
❑ Broad expertise and collaboration are required to solve the issue.
❑ The group is primarily made up of organizations, not individuals.
❑ The organizations' missions align with the group's goals.
❑ The organizations are committed to achieve the group's mission.
❑ The organizations are actively engaged in a collaborative process.
❑ The organizations are committed to democratic decision-making procedures.
❑ The organizations share or obtain resources to assist with the group's work.
❑ The organizations focus on education, advocacy and action on behalf of a specific population or issue.
❑ The group has non-profit status or claims it from an umbrella agency.

If you checked most of these items, the group may very likely be a coalition. To confirm, further study will be needed.

Now that you have decided to build or join an existing coalition, the next section will guide you in building an effective one.

RECAP

- ✓ Learn what collaboration can do to make an impact on issues that your community cares about.
- ✓ Decide on the kind of collaboration that is needed.
- ✓ Describe the purpose of the collaboration.
- ✓ Know why coalitions form and how they are supposed to work.
- ✓ Conduct a community assessment to decide if coalition building is the best approach.
- ✓ Develop a strategy for dealing with competing groups and coalitions.

Collaboration Resources

The Power of Collaborative Solutions: Six Principles and Effective Tools for Building Healthy Communities, by **Tom Wolff** addresses current social problems by helping people of diverse backgrounds work together to solve community challenges. The clear principles, illustrative stories, and practical tools show how to make lasting change happen.

Prevention is Primary: Strategies for Community Well Being, by **Larry** Cohen, **Vivian Chavez**, and **Sana Chemini** is a practical text that describes the overarching principles guiding prevention efforts, with a focus on social justice, health equity, and community resilience.

PART II
Build It!

BUILD YOUR CAMPFIRE

Once you have a site selected, it's time to build your fire.

Gathering Your Fuel

For a good fire, carefully select three items: tinder, kindling, and fuel wood.

- ✓ **Tinder.** Your fire starts from tinder, which is about as big around as a needle or string. It is any dry, shredded material such as cedar bark, grass, pine needles, milkweed fluff, or wood shavings.
- ✓ **Kindling.** Once tinder has caught fire, its heat can get larger pieces burning. Kindling is often splinters of wood or small twigs ranging from the size of a matchstick to the size of a pencil that can be snapped by hand. Whittle away damp bark before using sticks. Add them slowly, smaller ones first, building from tiny flames to small ones, and then healthy ones.
- ✓ **Fuel wood.** Fuel wood doesn't need to be any bigger around than your forearm. If possible, collect hardwood that snaps and breaks, but even damp fuel wood will burn because it will dry out and combust. Collect twice as much wood as you think you'll need, or the fire will go out while you're looking for more. Sort and pile it in increasingly large pieces in the order you will feed the fire.

1
TINDER

2
KINDLING

3
FUEL WOOD

Building Your Fire

The way you assemble wood before lighting it is called the *fire lay*. A few methods are recommended, depending on the fire's intended use. Build up, not out, to create a higher rather than flatter pile of wood.

- ✓ **A-Frame.** Make the letter "*A*" out of large kindling or small fuel wood (about 12" long and 1–2" diameter). The sides of the *A* rest on the floor of the fire pit; the "crossbar" rests on top of the sides. Put tinder inside the top triangle of the *A* so the twigs lean against the *A*'s crossbar making a miniature lean-to. Don't pack tinder too closely—leave enough space for good ventilation.

- ✓ **Teepee.** This is the most useful and easiest fire to light. It produces a fast flame and falls into itself in a pile of coals. The heat is directed to a single point and is useful for single-pot cooking. Once the teepee collapses, fuel wood can be laid around it in a log cabin style or crisscrossed on top of the flames. The key is to put a few sticks in the ground to support the rest of the kindling.

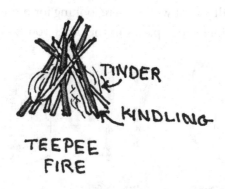

✓ **Log Cabin.** This makes good coals and has a classic campfire look. Getting it lit is challenging, since it's hard to access the interior. You can add wood to a teepee fire to make it a log cabin.

LOG CABIN
FIRE

✓ **Council Fire.** This fire takes bigger logs and is meant for entertaining crowds. It maintains good flames for a long time without adding more wood, since burning fuel drops down onto the larger logs and ignites them. Unlike a log cabin fire, no structural collapse should occur with a council fire.

COUNCIL FIRE

BUILD YOUR COALITION!

Just as a campfire needs to be planned with the right fire lay and fuel in mind, a coalition needs to have the right structure, organizations, and resources on board to make things work. The following recommendations will be detailed in part II to help you organize your coalition for success:

- Clarify the purpose, vision, and mission of the coalition
- Choose the simplest structure that will achieve your goals
- Involve the right people and organizations
- Grow transformational leaders
- Put commitments in writing
- Use effective communication strategies

Clarify the Purpose, Vision, and Mission of the Coalition

Not everyone has a similar view of what "collaboration" means. True collaboration requires a commitment to shared goals; a jointly developed structure and shared responsibility; mutual authority; accountability for success; community assessment; and sharing of resources, risks, and rewards. One of the key purposes for creating a coalition is to collaborate, but take the time to discuss with your members what collaboration really entails. In other words, collaboration means sharing a common vision for the future of your community. It means not always getting your own way, but developing a consensus about the best way. It means taking a chance that a strategy will succeed, or that a partner organization will follow through on its commitment. Once your members are comfortable with the general concept of collaboration, you are ready to take it a step further and develop vision and mission statements.

A clear vision and mission helps generate support and awareness for the coalition, identify partners, reduce conflict, and minimize time costs and distractions from appropriate actions (Butterfoss 2007, 223). Just as you must decide the purpose of a campfire, the best way to clarify your coalition's mission is to have members openly discuss the reasons that they want to build a coalition and what they think this organization of organizations can accomplish. This often occurs after a SWOT analysis is performed (see the previous chapter) or at the start of a strategic planning process, but it can be done anytime. The *process* of developing the mission and vision may be as critical as the *product* itself. Having a common vision and vocabulary enables members to talk about the issues, share common understanding, and decide what is expected and how to proceed.

Vision statement. The vision statement provides a picture of the desired future, described as if it were happening now (Campbell, Devine and Young 1990, 49). *Vision statements* are:

- ✓ Inspiring and uplifting
- ✓ Understood and shared by community members
- ✓ Broad enough to include diverse viewpoints and are easily communicated

For example: *Smoke Free York is a community where all residents are healthy and tobacco free!*

If coalition members have difficulty developing a mission statement, you can have them create a set of *value statements* or shared principles that will drive the coalition's work.

Value statements. These are core principles that focus on equity and how culture affects health and quality of life. By creating value statements, community members recognize their power and capacity to solve their own health issues. These statements then may be used to craft a formal mission statement. Consider the following:

- We value high standards of ethics and integrity.
- We value growth, creativity, and learning.
- We value open, honest relationships and communication.
- We value diversity.
- We value being able to do more with less.

Mission statement. A mission statement describes the purpose of the collaboration—the fundamental reason for its existence. It should capture what coalition members intend to do together to achieve the organizational vision. Every member should know the mission statement "by heart" and use it to recruit embers and communicate the coalition's accomplishments. An effective mission statement:

✓ Is concise; gets the point across in one brief sentence
✓ Is outcome-oriented and focuses on work that the coalition will do
✓ Is inspirational and inclusive
✓ Does not limit community sectors or strategies that may be involved

An example of a good mission statement is: *Safe Kids Kansas is a nonprofit coalition of organizations and businesses dedicated to prevent accidental injuries to children from birth to fourteen.*

Slogan or byline. A slogan or byline is a short phrase that is used to brand the coalition or market it to the public. It is often used as a brief mission statement that appears in campaigns, logos, or printed coalition material and products. An example is *Immunize to save lives.*

Coalition logos. Powerful causes, like those espoused by community coalitions, need powerful brands. Branding should influence the entire coalition; staff and members should use the logo whenever possible to reinforce the coalition's identity and mission. Deciding on a name and logo for the coalition are activities that can engage members and lead to early outcomes or "quick wins." A consensus method or contest can give each member an equal voice in the decision. A graphic artist may produce a more professional logo or catchy name, but the social capital that is built by a do-it-yourself process is invaluable. Keep in mind that the best names and logos are simple, easily recognizable and understandable, and can be easily reproduced in one or two-color print. A good rule of thumb is to imagine what the logo and name would look like on an envelope, as well as a T-shirt or banner.

Goals. Goals are dreams with deadlines. The coalition will develop goals for each issue that it addresses. Goal setting is energizing; it encourages discussion, reveals differences of opinion, and builds consensus. Further, goals are:

- ✓ Broad descriptions of desired outcomes that emerge from the mission statement
- ✓ Long range, but tangible and attainable
- ✓ Used to specify priority actions for the coalition and its work groups

An example of a goal is *"To improve health care provider knowledge and practices concerning patient's self-management of asthma."* A coalition likely will develop a work group to focus on each goal. Work groups can then develop specific objectives to address these goals.

Choose the Simplest Structure that Achieves Your Goals

Coalitions require time and resources, so keep your coalition structure and reporting procedures as simple as possible. Coalitions may focus so much on creating procedures that they fail to carry out their action plans. A coalition's structure should fit its goals and resources and be no more complex than necessary. Form should follow function to ensure that the coalition is flexible and responsive.

Certain internal structures help ensure coalition effectiveness and durability, such as vision and mission statements, action plans, role and job descriptions, bylaws, steering committees, work groups, and written records (agenda, minutes, rosters, and reports). Studies show that when coalitions are structured and task oriented, they are perceived as more effective by members and staff (Butterfoss and Kegler 2009, 257). Administrative tasks, such as producing minutes and informative materials, are the "glue" that makes it possible for multiple, diverse partners to develop synergy and work efficiently together (Lasker et al. 2001, 182).

Does Size Matter? People often ask how big is too big for a community coalition. Optimal coalition size varies according to its stage of development, its mission, what it needs to accomplish, and whether it represents an urban-, rural-, or county-level population.

Pros and cons can be identified for large versus small coalitions. Larger coalitions have more people to manage the workload, divide responsibilities, and provide diverse perspectives on issues. However, meetings are more difficult to schedule and facilitate, and every member may not be engaged in a meaningful activity. In smaller coalitions, communication and interaction are easier, and personal satisfaction is enhanced from constant and meaningful involvement. However, heavier workloads may lead to burnout and key points of view might not be represented (Andringa and Engstrom 2001, 75).

Most coalitions start with a smaller group of organizations and expand as appropriate to accomplish their goals. The size of a coalition is not critical; rather, it is how the coalition is *organized and managed* that matters. If the group is large, then the work must be divided among committees or work groups in order to be efficient. Work groups can be subdivided into teams that have specific tasks to accomplish.

Coalition governance. How the coalition is governed matters. Coalitions may be too structured and hierarchical or too democratic—both situations lead to slow progress (Garza 2005, 18). Challenges, such as the availability of community resources, scope and intensity of strategies, balance of work between volunteers and paid staff, interorganizational relationships, and external factors that are beyond the coalition's control, make good management and governance critical. Leaders and staff members must learn to share the work, acknowledge that most tasks will be more complicated than imagined, focus on priorities, and learn to adapt within a dynamic environment (Bazzoli et al. 2003, 63S). While no single governance structure is the "right" model, evaluating whether the governance structure is working is essential. If the structure is not working, the coalition should feel free to change it.

Two main governance models exist for coalitions: The Lead Agency Model and the Independent Nonprofit Model. For the Lead Agency Model, any health department, hospital, academic institution, or other non-profit agency can assume the lead agent role. One agency may convene the coalition, and another serve as the fiscal agent; or one agency may provide all services—convene the coalition and then provide office and/or meeting space, staff, communications support, and fiscal oversight. In both cases, staff manages the coalition, and an elected steering committee provides leadership and oversight. The organizational chart might look like this:

Lead Agency Coalition Model

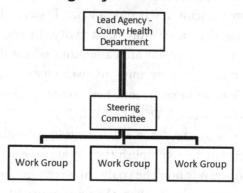

A strong lead agency should:

- Be linked to and respected by local community organizations and key leaders
- Have a deep understanding of community health issues, priority populations, and local politics
- Commit to collaboration and shared decision making
- Demonstrate positive practices that support coalition activities, such as clean indoor air policies
- Serve as an umbrella organization to provide not-for-profit status (501 c 3) for the coalition
- Support the coalition's administrative and resource needs
- Provide and/or hire coalition staff through its employment and benefits structure
- Use its development, media, and advocacy capabilities to promote coalition and its work

In the Independent Nonprofit Model, the coalition has non-profit, 501(c) 3 status and manages itself, as shown in the following graphic:

Independent Nonprofit—501 (c) 3—Model

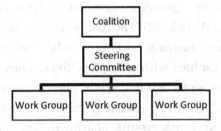

To qualify for non-profit status, the coalition must have:

- A written mission statement, goals, and bylaws
- An executive board or steering committee
- A record-keeping system for minutes, financial, and other reports
- A budget, accounting system, and annual audits
- IRS-determined federal tax exempt status (via articles of incorporation)
- State and local tax exemptions filed for income, sales, and property taxes
- Adherence to state, county and municipal charitable solicitation laws regarding advocacy and lobbying
- An IRS employer identification number
- Registration with the state unemployment insurance bureau
- Directors' or officers' liability insurance

The executive board or steering committee. In both models, a common approach to coalition governance is to form an executive board or steering committee to research issues and make recommendations and time-sensitive decisions. The committee usually meets three to four times per year for orientation and training, networking and linking work groups, strategic planning, and evaluation. It is composed of officers of the coalition (chair, past chair, vice-chair, secretary-treasurer), chairs, and even vice-chairs of action-focused work groups, and, perhaps, at-large members. The steering committee may develop from the core group that originally organized the coalition or be elected from the general membership.

Even though steering committee members are elected to represent coalition members, they should not have undue influence on decision

making. One effective course of action is to outline the roles and responsibilities of the steering committee members, staff members, leaders, and
officers (Coalitions Work 2012). The coalition also may identify the types
of decisions that can be made without members' vote or consent, such
as funding opportunities with short deadlines, unexpected legislative
actions, or other decisions that may not be appropriate for broad dissemi-
nation due to their sensitive nature (e.g., conflicts among key partners).

Work groups and task groups. Sharing the coalition's tasks among
work groups of approximately ten to fifteen members is most efficient.
Smaller task groups should have at least three members to provide
enough capacity and diversity of thought to complete the tasks assigned
(Walker and Heard 2011, 505). Although no more than four work groups
are advisable, the number should be determined by the coalition's goals,
as well as the ability of staff members and leaders to efficiently manage
them (i.e., plan, facilitate, and execute follow-up activities).

Work groups can be developed to concentrate the work around
specific topic areas that the coalition addresses. For example, in an
immunization coalition, work groups could be organized to focus on
specific age groups (e.g., infant and childhood, adolescent, and adult
immunization) or activities (e.g., public awareness, policy and legislation,
provider education, and access to care). For a multiple-issue coalition,
work groups naturally fall into topical areas. For example, a minority
health coalition might have work groups organized according to various health disparities such as cancer, diabetes, HIV/AIDS, and infant
mortality. Similarly, an injury -prevention coalition might organize its
work groups around poison prevention, playground safety, fire safety,
and motor vehicle safety.

For statewide coalitions or rural coalitions spread over one or more
counties, work groups might be organized geographically with each one
covering similar topics for a specific community or geographic area.
Ultimately, each coalition should divide its work rationally and in ways
that are efficient and manageable. Providing rosters of work groups and
their members, as well as electronic mailing lists can increase cohesion
and internal member-to-member communication.

Work groups may be organized on an open membership basis in which
a core of members is maintained from year to year. Members rotate off as

desired and new members are added as they show interest. However, some coalitions start the year by disbanding all groups and reforming ones that are still needed. An assessment process helps the coalition to reassess its composition and refocus the work group, if necessary. This approach can reduce stagnation, improve flexibility and future orientation, and provide new leadership opportunities (Bobowick et al 2001, 12).

If work groups expand due to the interest and commitment of new members, they can break into task groups to accomplish specific tasks in a timely manner. For example, if a work group convenes around bullying in schools; one task group might focus on community assessment while another might organize a training seminar for teachers, coaches, and school administrators. To encourage smooth-functioning work, see **TOOL 3: Coalition Guidelines.**

TOOL 3: Coalition Guidelines

✓ Develop an annual schedule of meetings, set a year in advance.
✓ Circulate agendas//support materials to members before meetings.
✓ Maintain complete and accurate minutes of all meetings.
✓ Keep meetings brief and well-focused.
✓ Prepare written roles/responsibilities for work and task group members.
✓ Assign work based on background, expertise, and schedules of members.
✓ Distribute tasks so that everyone participates, but no one is overloaded.
✓ Monitor members' work and assure that tasks are completed.
✓ Acknowledge members' contributions in meetings, minutes, and newsletters.
✓ If possible, have staff member liaison with each work group.

Bylaws. Bylaws are the formal, written rules that help a coalition define its purpose and the practical details of governing itself. They serve as legal guidelines and have to be filed with the secretary of state of the state in which the non-profit group is incorporated or registered. Bylaws enable members to determine the rules that they will abide by. These rules ensure stability, continuity, and structure, especially during times of rapid growth or transition. Bylaws are different from policies and procedures that focus on day-to-day operations. Bylaws outline the group's official name, purpose, membership requirements, election and voting processes, and member and leader responsibilities. Beware of including more detail than is needed; if bylaws need to be amended, a formal vote of the membership is required.

Having bylaws can be helpful to any coalition or partnership, regardless of size or purpose. Coalitions may start out with a simple set of guidelines until they are ready to adopt formal bylaws. According to the Community Tool Box website, bylaws should be written when the coalition 1) needs to clarify its purpose, elections, or other operational matters; 2) changes its purpose or the way it operates; or 3) applies for nonprofit status. While they do not solve all problems, bylaws provide a process for ensuring equality, fairness, and consistency and reducing conflict of interest and lack of focus or productive activity (Heimlich and Dresbach 2004, 2). **TOOL 4: Coalition Bylaws Template** can serve as the foundation of a coalition bylaws document.

TOOL 4: Coalition Bylaws Template

Bylaws of _____

Article I - Name, Purpose
- Section 1: The name of the organization shall be _____.
- Section 2: The _____ is organized exclusively for charitable, scientific, and educational purposes, more specifically to _____.

Article II – Membership
Membership shall consist of any community member who adheres to the Coalition's mission.

Article III - Annual Meeting
- Section 1: Annual Meeting. The date, time and place of the annual meeting shall be set by the steering committee.
- Section 2: Special Meetings. Special meetings may be called by the chair or any officer.
- Section 3: Notice. Notice of each meeting shall be given to each voting member, by mail, not less than ten days before the meeting.

TOOL 4: Coalition Bylaws Template

Article IV – Steering Committee

- Section 1: Committee Role, Size, Compensation. The steering committee is responsible for overall policy and direction of the Coalition and delegates responsibility for day-to-day operations to the coalition director and work groups. The committee shall have up to ___ members who receive no compensation other than expenses.

- Section 2: Meetings. The steering committee shall meet at least ___, at an agreed upon time and place.

- Section 3: Elections. Election of new or current members to a second term will be an item of business at the Coalition's annual meeting. Members will be elected by a majority vote of the Coalition.

- Section 4: Terms. Members shall serve _-year terms, but are eligible for re-election.

- Section 5: Quorum. A quorum must be attended by at least ___ percent of the members before business can be transacted or motions made.

- Section 6: Notice. An official meeting requires that members have written notice ten days in advance.

- Section 7. Officers and Duties. The five officers of the Coalition consist of a chair, past chair, vice chair, secretary and treasurer who are designated as the executive committee. Their duties are:

  o Chair shall convene regularly scheduled meetings, shall preside or arrange for other officers to preside at each meeting in this order: vice-chair, secretary and treasurer.

  o Vice-Chair will chair committees on special subjects as decided by the board.

  o Secretary shall keep records of committee actions, which include sending out meeting announcements, taking/distributing minutes and agenda to members, and assuring that records are maintained.

  o Treasurer shall report at board meetings. S/He shall chair the finance committee, assist in preparing the budget, develop fundraising plans, and make financial information available to Coalition and the public.

- Section 8: Vacancies. When a steering committee vacancy occurs, nominations for new members may be received from Coalition members by the secretary two weeks in advance of a meeting. Nominations shall be sent to members with the steering committee meeting announcement for vote at the next meeting. Vacancies will be filled only to the end of the involved member's term.

TOOL 4: Coalition Bylaws Template

- Section 9: Resignation, Termination and Absences. Resignation from the steering committee must be in writing to the secretary. Members may be dropped for excess absences (if they have three unexcused absences from meetings in a year) or removed for other reasons by a three-quarter vote of other members.
- Section 10: Special Meetings. Special meetings shall be called at request of the chair or one third of the steering committee. Notices of special meetings shall be sent to members two weeks in advance.

Article V – Work Groups
- Section 1: The steering committee may create work groups as needed. Work group chairs are voted on by members.
- Section 2: The officers serve as members of the executive committee. Except for the power to amend Articles of Incorporation and Bylaws, the board shall have all the powers and authority of the Coalition during intervals between general Coalition meetings.
- Section 3: Finance Committee. The treasurer chairs the finance committee, which includes three other board members. The committee develops and reviews fiscal procedures, a fundraising plan, and annual budget with staff and other board members. The board must approve the budget; all expenditures must be within the budget. Any major change in the budget must be approved by the steering committee. The fiscal year shall be the calendar year. Annual reports are required to be submitted to the steering committee showing expenditures, income, and pending income. Financial records are public information and shall be made available to the public, Coalition members and steering committee.

Article VI – Amendments
Bylaws may be amended by a two-thirds majority of the Coalition. Proposed amendments must be submitted to the secretary and sent out with regular Coalition meeting announcements. These bylaws were approved at a meeting of the board of directors of _____ on _____, 20XX.

Involve the Right Individuals and Organizations

If your coalition plans to implement widespread change, your efforts should include the top leaders from relevant organizations. In our campfire analogy, we discussed the benefits of selecting several kinds of wood for your fire—tinder, kindling, and fuel wood—and how woods burn at different temperatures. The same is true for coalitions; diverse representation and engagement from local government, schools, businesses, and non-profit organizations will ensure that your strategies are carried out efficiently and effectively. Try visualizing the coalition as a mirror that reflects the rich diversity of the community it serves. Partners must be trustworthy and credible, and must have mutual goals, expertise, and resources.

Recruit diverse members. How do you know if you have the right people on board? A diverse membership has a range of stakeholders invested in or affected by your coalition's issue(s) and is representative of your community (Foster-Fishman et al. 2001, 249). Other dimensions of diversity include age; education level; ethnicity; family status; gender; income; military experience; national, regional, or other geographical areas of origin; ownership of property and assets; physical and mental ability; race; sexual orientation; social class; spiritual practice; and work experience (Lolly 2005, 1).

These "community-committed" coalitions create climates in which diverse members share power, knowledge, and access to the coalition (Wolff 2001, 275). Meaningful participation can extend beyond physical involvement to include generation of ideas, contributions to decision making, and sharing of responsibility (CTSA, 2011):

- ✓ We discuss diversity and how to incorporate it into the work.
- ✓ We celebrate differences in food, customs and culture.
- ✓ We schedule meetings at convenient times and places for all.
- ✓ We offer transportation, childcare, and translation services.
- ✓ We use inclusive and valuing language that is free from professional jargon or acronyms.
- ✓ We orient new members.
- ✓ We provide opportunities for leadership on many levels with appropriate training.
- ✓ We schedule time for socializing.

TOOL 5: Inclusivity Checklist can help you assess how inclusive your coalition is (Rosenthal 1995).

TOOL 5: Inclusivity Checklist

How prepared are you for multicultural work? Check each statement that applies to your coalition. If you can't check a box, this might be an area to change.

- ❑ The leadership of our coalition is multiracial and multicultural.
- ❑ We recruit members who represent the diversity of our community.
- ❑ We cultivate new leaders, particularly people of color.
- ❑ Our mission, process and products reflect contributions of diverse cultural and social groups.
- ❑ Members of diverse cultural and social groups participate in all aspects of our work.
- ❑ Meetings are not dominated by speakers from any one group.
- ❑ All segments of our community are represented in decision making.
- ❑ We are sensitive to and aware of different religious/cultural holidays, customs and food preferences.
- ❑ We communicate clearly; people of different cultures share their opinions and participate in meetings.
- ❑ We prohibit ethnic, racial, and sexual stereotypes and prejudicial comments, slurs, or jokes.

Your membership should reflect the special needs and issues relevant to your coalition's mission. For example, a chronic disease prevention coalition would recruit members who represent the diseases (e.g., cancer, diabetes, cardiovascular disease) that are prevalent in the community. One way is to decide what sectors of the community should be involved in your coalition and then analyze your membership to determine whether you have engaged diverse organizations from those sectors. The sectors will vary depending on your issue, but might include the following:

- **Community at large:** Community-wide efforts that impact social/built environments, such as food access, safe walking/biking routes and tobacco-free ordinances
- **Schools:** All private and public learning institutions, such as preschool, elementary, middle, and high schools, colleges and universities

- **Worksites:** Places of employment—restaurants, retail establishments, or private or government offices
- **Healthcare institutions:** Places where people receive treatment, preventive care or emergency services—hospitals, physicians' offices, or clinics
- **Community-based organizations (CBOs):** Groups or organizations that provide human services—childcare settings, faith-based organizations, and senior centers

Once you identify the necessary sectors, you can decide what organizations within those sectors would be appropriate given the work that you have set out to do. These questions may help you make that determination:

- Who has previously supported issue?
- Which organizations have compatible goals with yours?
- What prior relationships exist among these organizations?
- What are their values and cultures?
- What do they offer (resources, power, and results)?
- What are their public records/positions about the issue?

TOOL 6: Coalition Membership Gap Analysis describes participative member "gap analysis" and serves as the basis for further recruitment.

Recruitment methods and messages. Coalition recruitment is an ongoing process: if your coalition is not actively recruiting new organizations and ideas, you risk becoming obsolete. New members can revitalize a group that has grown stagnant or no longer sees issues clearly. Adopt an open-door membership policy that builds on diversity and new ideas, while approaching new organizations and individuals with full awareness of their capabilities and resources.

Use a variety of recruitment methods; you are limited only by your creativity:

- Introduce your coalition and the opportunities for membership via an introductory letter, telephone call, or e-mail, followed by a face-to-face meeting.

TOOL 6: Coalition Membership Gap Analysis

1. Update and access your roster of members
2. Decide what community sectors you will engage; adapt this list:
   - Health/medical
   - Government/legislative
   - Business/labor/employment
   - Religious/faith-based
   - Local community
   - Recreational organizations/facilities
   - Nutrition/food services
   - Family/children/youth/elderly
   - Health advocacy/medical Issues
   - Professional/trade associations
   - Other interest groups
3. For each sector, write category on a flip chart sheet and mount the sheets on the wall. Define each sector and provide examples of organizations in each.
4. Create name badges (print from computer or use index cards) of current member organizations. Distribute to members attending a steering committee or general coalition meeting.
5. Have members affix their cards/name tags to applicable sheets.
6. Sit down; observe the results. Some sheets will be full, while others will be empty or have only one or two entries. If you have more than one member from each organization, use a one organization: one vote policy to assure that power is shared equally.
7. Either all together or in small groups, brainstorm organizations for the sparse sectors. The phone book or local Chamber of Commerce or small business rosters may get you started. Identify what role each organization will play in the coalition; that is, Why are they valuable to our efforts? What are benefits of partnering?
8. Choose members and volunteers to contact the organizations to start recruiting representatives. The coordinator may then follow up with membership information about the coalition and face-face contact with each organization.

- Develop a connection through another organization that you belong to.
- Stimulate interest from community members via a community assessment, town meeting, or survey.
- Identify potential partners at a conference or training.

Key recruitment messages follow here:

- Many organizations working together can achieve more than one organization can alone!
- Involving diverse member organizations helps build community buy-in and consensus!
- With your participation and expertise, we will build credibility and influence!
- Does our community work as it should? Can we engage in a new way to be healthier, safer, better?

The recruiter should describe how the potential organization can contribute and why its participation is needed. Certain groups or individuals should be recruited early in the life of the coalition because they are good organizers or planners. Some organizations, such as businesses or parent groups, are better recruited later when definitive tasks need to be done.

Retaining Members. People join coalitions for many reasons—they may want to build new social or professional relationships, accomplish critical goals, have influence and impact, or just want to be informed and "in the know." Find out what motivates them to join and, ultimately, stay involved. Individuals and organizations are more likely to sustain their involvement when they:

- Have positive social interactions
- Have access to information and resources
- Receive recognition for their contributions
- Can influence decision making
- Get adequate orientation and training
- Experience varied and fulfilling opportunities to participate
- See positive outcomes from their efforts (Butterfoss 2007)

Linking veteran members to new recruits can be an effective recruitment and retention method. It's much harder to say no to another volunteer, and connecting with other members may increase the likelihood of becoming engaged in the coalition sooner and more fully. If you initially involve members in activities that fit their talents and interests, you can encourage them to be more involved as their comfort and trust levels with your coalition and its members grows. **TOOL 8: The Buddy Method for Recruitment** may be useful in your coalition for mentoring new members.

TOOL 8: The Buddy Method for Recruitment

Step 1: Each time a new strategy is introduced, the chair asks members to consider, "Who is not at the table that might help us enact this strategy or idea?"

Step 2: For each identified organization, a member who has the best connection to that organization is asked to begin the recruitment process and volunteer to be the "buddy."

Step 3: The buddy contacts the prospective member and asks him or her to join the coalition effort. The buddy encourages and answers immediate questions about the coalition or volunteering. Contact information is forwarded to the chair or coalition director.

Step 4: The director follows up with a phone call, and sends an orientation packet to the prospective member with key information about the coalition and its work.

Step 5: When the buddy receives notice of the next coalition meeting, he or she phones the recruit to ensure that the notice was received and encourages the new member to attend. Transportation and other needs also are arranged.

Step 6: At the meeting, the buddy greets the member, helps acclimate him or her to the meeting protocol and introduces him or her to others. The recruit is given an opportunity to introduce him or herself to the group. The chair offers a personal welcome.

Providing orientation sessions, either in person or online and downloadable member orientation packets, as detailed in **TOOL 7: Member Orientation Packet,** also are helpful.

TOOL 7: Member Orientation Packet	
✓ Coalition history	✓ Steering committee and work group members
✓ Vision, mission, and goals	✓ Sample meeting minutes
✓ Organizational chart	✓ Meeting and events calendar
✓ Bylaws and coalition guidelines	✓ Newspaper article or success story
✓ Roster of members	✓ Coalition product or tool

Member Roles. Partners in collaborations play varied roles at different times (Himmelman 2002, 10-13). Members may assume any one or more of the following potential roles:

- **Convener/facilitator**—encourages discussion on issue(s) that may lead to further action
- **Catalyst**—uses organization's influence and resources to encourage others to "get on board" with the coalition and its issue(s) and participate in long-term problem solving
- **Funder or conduit**—provides funds or serves as a channel for funding
- **Advocate**—actively supports individuals and groups that are the coalition's priority and/or promotes policy and systems changes that emerge from the coalition's work.
- **Community organizer**—conducts ongoing recruitment and engages community-based organizations and individuals in the work
- **Technical assistance provider**—provides training and expertise on planning, data collection, funding proposals, legal issues, marketing, advocacy, and other subjects
- **Capacity builder**—helps organizations and individuals prioritize issues and secure resources to map community assets, set goals, evaluate activities, and access resources
- **Partner**—shares risks, responsibilities, and rewards; builds trusting relationships; values others' viewpoints; and identifies challenges so that others share in their solutions

Grow Transformational Leaders

*If your actions inspire others to dream more, learn more,
do more and become more, you are a leader.*
—John Quincy Adams

Every successful organization has effective leadership at its core. Likewise, good leadership is an essential ingredient of coalitions and partnerships. Effective coalition leaders facilitate productive interactions among partners by spanning organizational boundaries and overcoming barriers that limit creative thinking and action. Such leaders create an environment that is efficient and task oriented, and fosters high levels of member satisfaction and commitment (Butterfoss 2007, 109). Coalitions require a delicate balance of leadership that is neither bureaucratic nor autocratic. It starts with a founding organization that is rooted in the values of community, collaboration, and diversity. This organization creates the conditions that make principled leadership possible and foster the emergence of capable, visionary leaders. Those leaders, whether paid or voluntary, have members' interests at heart and are able to effectively share their vision for a better community.

Coalition leadership should be diverse, broad-based, and shared, or *collaborative*. In collaborative leadership, individuals who are part of a group take turns leading the organization. Over a hundred years ago, the great sociologist Max Weber said that organizations that will survive and thrive will be those that foster *acts of leadership* throughout the system, rather than assuming that leaders exist only at the top (Dourado 2007, 96).

If we start thinking about "acts of leadership" rather than "actual leaders," we can build a team, organization, or coalition that is overflowing with collaborative leadership that will be sustained over time. As the following table shows, collaborative leaders build relationships and bridges to create more leaders (The Turning Point 2006).

Collaborative leaders help others learn from their mistakes and share that learning. They use supportive and inclusive methods to engage the community. And, finally, they share power to set priorities, share resources, and evaluate performance. Ironically, the more that power is shared, the more there is to use.

Collaborative versus Traditional Leadership

Traditional Leadership	Collaborative Leadership
Top down	Self-governing
Few make decisions	Broad participation
Unilateral action	Guide and coordinate process
Win or shift power	Build relationships
Linear thinking	Systems thinking
Programs and products	Process
Charisma	Vision
Persuasive	Empathetic
Group falls apart if leader leaves	Group continues if leader leaves

Collaborative leaders need, or should develop, certain critical skills and capacities. The Turning Point Leadership Development Collaborative was a partnership of local, state, and national public health organizations that worked to increase collaborative leadership in public health practice. The collaborative identified six key elements unique to the practice of leading a collaborative organization or process (Nicola 2013):

1. **Assess the environment for collaboration:** Understand the context for change before you act.
2. **Create clarity:** Use visioning to define shared values and engage people in positive action.
3. **Build trust:** Create safe places for developing shared purpose and action.
4. **Share power and influence:** Develop the synergy of people, organizations, and communities to accomplish more.
5. **Develop people:** Commit to develop people as your key asset through mentoring and coaching.
6. **Self-reflect:** Understand your own leadership and engage others.

One type of collaborative leadership is transformational leadership (also called servant or facilitative leadership) in which leaders are able to inspire followers to accomplish great things; also, leaders and members are inextricably linked in this transformation process (Burns 1978, 20). Transformational leaders are change agents who create and articulate a clear vision, empower followers to achieve at higher standards, lead as peer problem solvers, and build broad-based involvement and participation aimed at transforming the organization and/or community around them (Northouse 2013). In other words, transformational leaders become leaders to *do something*, not to *be someone*. For example, Nelson Mandela's vision and persistence resulted in monumental changes in governance that transformed the entire nation of South Africa. Likewise, Ryan White raised awareness about AIDS and became a spokesperson for increasing federal funding of AIDS research.

Leadership may be visualized as a continuum that moves from laissez-faire (non-interference) to transactional leadership (exchange process between leaders and followers) to transformational leadership, as shown below (Bass 1985, 21).

Leadership Continuum

Laissez-faire → Transactional → Transformational

Transformational leaders usually exhibit one or more of the following four characteristics:

1. Charisma or idealized influence or high standards of ethical conduct that make others want to follow their vision and emulate them
2. Inspirational motivation or high expectations that inspire or motivate others to become committed to the organization's shared vision
3. Intellectual stimulation or the ability to stimulate others to be innovative and challenge their own beliefs and values to solve problems, as well as those of the leader and the organization

4. Individualized consideration or the ability to listen to and support the needs of others and act as coaches to help them become actualized or empowered (Bass 1985, 22)

The following figure shows how transformational leadership leads to greater effects than transactional leadership (adapted from Northouse 2013, 189).

Transformational Leadership

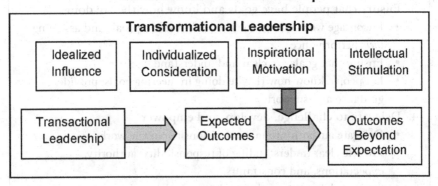

Transformational leadership is useful in coalitions because it acknowledges leadership as a mutual process that occurs between leaders and followers, and focuses not only on exchanging rewards, but also on attention to others' needs and growth. To find out whether you or your coalition leaders are transformational, review the following Ten Traits of Transformational Leaders (Northouse 2013, 186-189) and then complete **TOOL 9: Am I a Transformational Leader?** (Ohio Resource Literacy Center, 2013).

Different leadership skills may be required during different stages of coalition development. While younger coalitions may require greater facilitation and listening skills to recruit and engage diverse members, negotiation and advocacy skills may be needed to bring about more complex environmental changes later on (Roussos and Fawcett 2000, 375). Since leadership is so critical to an organization's success, coalitions must commit to identifying a corps of emerging, skilled community leaders if capacity is to be built.

Ten Traits of Transformational Leaders

1. **Let go of things others can do**
   - Let go of authority to make decisions about the work.
   - Know what others in the group can/want to do.
   - Build people's skills to lead by involving them in the work.

2. **Encourage initiative, ideas, and risk taking**
   - Actively seek ideas and suggestions from the work group.
   - Allow people to run with ideas, even if it involves some risk.
   - Be careful not to put down or discount ideas.

3. **Ensure that people have goals and know how they're doing**
   - Encourage work groups to take lead in setting goals and assessing *their* performance.
   - Ensure that goals are clear and understandable.
   - Let people know how they're doing in meeting goals; provide guidance and support.

4. **Delegate to challenge, develop, and empower**
   - Delegate authority to make decisions about the work.
   - Provide clear understanding of responsibility, authority, expectations, and constraints.
   - Support delegation within and outside the work group.

5. **Coach to ensure success**
   - Set up controls that monitor progress, but aren't seen as restrictive.
   - Coach before a person begins a task or assumes responsibility, and also coach along the way.
   - Use coaching to guide and instruct others, while maintaining and enhancing their self-esteem.

6. **Reinforce good work and good attempts**
   - Know what kind of reinforcement works best for each person; use verbal praise often.
   - Provide tangible reinforcement when possible (e.g., recognition letters, awards, or gifts)
   - Reinforce what someone does well even when his or her work has a few flaws

7. **Share information, knowledge, and skills**
   - Meet with your group regularly to share and update information
   - Make sure people have information necessary to achieve a task or responsibility or know how to get it.
   - Share members' insights, knowledge, expertise, and skills.

8. **Value, trust, and respect each individual**
   - Encourage others to take control of their jobs with authority to take action.
   - Recognize good work and creative ideas; don't minimize their contributions.
   - Listen to others; empathize with their problems and concerns.
9. **Provide support without taking over**
   - Understand that support is essential; know when it's needed. Support others (e.g., coach, reinforce, prepare for resistance, and gain commitment).
   - Resist temptation to take over when things go wrong.
10. **Practice what you preach**
   - Support others through rough spots of tasks instead of criticizing errors or taking over.
   - Ask for ideas and empower others to implement them, especially those that involve risk.
   - Tell others that they are important; show them through actions.

TOOL 9: Am I a Transformational Leader?	Yes	No
1. I let go of things others can do.	❏	❏
2. I encourage new ideas, problem-solving methods, and risk taking.	❏	❏
3. I ensure that people have goals and know how they're doing.	❏	❏
4. I delegate to challenge, develop, and empower others.	❏	❏
5. I coach others to ensure success.	❏	❏
6. I reinforce good work and attempts.	❏	❏
7. I share information, knowledge and skills.	❏	❏
8. I value, trust, and respect each individual.	❏	❏
9. I provide support without taking over.	❏	❏
10. I practice what I preach.	❏	❏

Planning for succession. By setting terms of office for leadership positions, the coalition grooms new leaders and gives them opportunities to manage smaller tasks and lead volunteers, while preparing for larger leadership roles. A succession plan also allows more leadership opportunities for other members and opens up the coalition to new ideas. Coalitions need to decide on term limits in advance (such as, one or two years), whether leaders can serve more than one term, and whether succession from vice-chair to chair should be planned. Experience with community and state-level coalitions favors one-year, renewable terms of office, since coalitions meet infrequently and leader orientation takes time.

Leader recruitment. Even though the benefits of developing and rotating leaders are clear, coalitions often struggle to find able leaders and sustain their involvement. Think about recruiting leaders in three categories: formal, voluntary and informal leaders.

- **Formal leaders** are the obvious recruits in any community—those who already hold visible leadership positions in mainstream organizations, such as CEOs of businesses, government and private institutions, and not-for-profit agencies. Although these leaders are savvy and experienced in management, they may be untested in collaborative decision-making environments or too busy to give the coalition the attention it needs.
- **Voluntary leaders** are those who hold leadership positions in voluntary, community-based organizations. They are also natural choices for leadership since they bring respect and tested leadership skills to the coalition. These leaders are more accustomed to working in a democratic decision-making environment, but also may more used to a board structure.
- **Informal leaders** usually have not held previous elected or appointed leadership positions. They represent the natural leadership and authentic voices of the community. By engaging them, coalition credibility is enhanced. Community members who may have been hesitant to join coalition efforts may be more likely to step forward and volunteer to help these leaders. Informal leaders are also invaluable sources of information in a community. Even if they do not hold elected office or regularly attend coalition meetings, they are in tune with the community, know other key stakeholders, and may mentor others to join and lead coalitions.

   Stimulating Leadership. How can coalitions encourage people to serve in leadership positions? Like members, leaders must perceive that the benefits of leadership outweigh the costs. When the potential leader is recruited, he or she already knows that certain costs will be incurred. For example, extra time will have to be spent in preparing for, traveling to, attending, and facilitating meetings, and extra responsibilities will be added to the leader's regular workload. Thus, coalition recruiters need to emphasize the benefits or "privileges" of leadership, such as opportunities to:

- Network with other leaders, movers and shakers
- Develop transferrable leadership skills, such as public speaking and facilitation
- Increase connection to community and coalition members
- Represent the coalition via print, radio, and televised media and community forums
- Travel to state/national meetings to represent the coalition
- Increase visibility and prominence for the leaders' organization
- Add leadership experience to resumes that require or value community service
- Obtain letters of reference and recommendation that attest to leadership ability
- Contribute to a worthwhile effort.

Put Commitments in Writing

   Just as no one would want to accept a position in which the responsibilities are not clearly described, no one wants to become a coalition member without knowing the responsibilities involved. Yet, coalitions often neglect this key aspect of member engagement. Later, coalition leaders and/or staff members may wonder why members fail to show up for meetings or follow through on tasks. One way to prevent this situation is to construct a simple "job description" for volunteers, like the one in **TOOL 10: Coalition Member Job Description**, and use it to orient them to their responsibilities.

TOOL 10: Coalition Member Job Description

✓ Prepare for and attend coalition and work group meetings regularly
✓ Gather/relay appropriate information to coalition as a basis for decision-making
✓ Help conduct community assessments and participate in strategic and action planning
✓ Share ideas/concerns and assure that others are invited to do the same
✓ Help carry out work group initiatives
✓ Serve as meeting recorder on rotating basis
✓ Report coalition progress to own organization and share its concerns/idea with coalition
✓ Be a coalition ambassador at other meetings/events
✓ Recruit other members
✓ Serve as an elected coalition leader
✓ Help develop resources to sustain coalition
✓ Advocate and promote the coalition's mission when/wherever possible

Time Commitment:
✓ Approximately one to three hours per month
✓ Attend work group/coalition meetings and major events
✓ One-year availability

Disagreements or uncertainty about commitments can derail any collaboration. Besides the volunteer job description in TOOL 10, a commitment letter or memorandum of understanding (MOU) can clarify the expectations of each organizational partner in the coalition. The MOU lays out the rules that govern your coalition, especially concerning substantial contributions that partners make to support your efforts. It includes vision, mission, and purpose; values and assumptions; timelines and milestones; expectations of leaders and members; contributions and roles; financial relationships; and rules on participation, decision making, communication, and conflict. You can use **TOOL 11: Memorandum of Understanding (MOU)** as a template.

TOOL 11: Memorandum of Understanding (MOU)

Introduction: Describe what the agreement will address. Identify each organization's qualifications, jurisdiction, and special expertise.

Purpose: Specify what will be accomplished by the agreement.

Authorities: Identify organizational signatories.

Roles and responsibilities:

Roles of each party in the agreement, including contractors

- Interests and areas of expertise of cooperating organizations
- Procedures for information sharing and confidentiality
- How comments, recommendations, and data from partner organizations will be used
- What commitments are involved regarding resources
- Anticipated schedule and timeline
- Expectations of either organization (e.g., credit, media issues)

Partner representatives who will oversee implementation of the agreement: (Usually enumerated in an attachment)

Administration of agreement:

- Describes how disagreements will be resolved
- Describes how the MOU may be modified or terminated
- Acknowledges that individual organizations' authority and responsibilities are not altered by the MOU

Use Effective Communication Strategies

Coalitions should use innovative methods to connect members to the coalition and to one another. Meeting agendas and minutes, annual reports, and community action plans will keep members abreast of coalition progress. Websites, electronic mailing lists, and social media tools such as Facebook, Twitter, and blogs are other essential communication tools.

Run effective meetings. Meetings can be good or bad. Bad meetings last forever, never seem to get to the point, and members wonder why they even attended. Effective ones leave them feeling accomplished and energized. The following tips may help you run more effective meetings:

- *Clarify the meeting's objective.* A meeting often is called without considering its outcome.
  o Do you want to make a decision or generate ideas?
  o Do you want to share information or train members?
  o Do you want to plan or monitor progress? (Mind Tools 2012).

To help you determine your meeting's objective, complete this sentence: By *meeting's end, I want the group to* _____.

- *Plan your meeting.* Invite the right people, set expectations with presenters, develop an agenda with expected outcomes for each item, and provide at least a week's notice and advance reading materials. Meetings should be held in neutral locations or rotated among convenient sites.
- *Use effective meeting methods.* The chair should: thank people for coming, review ground rules, introduce participants, review agenda items and time limits, and ask for questions. This provides structure and communicates that the meeting has a schedule and expected outcomes. Follow the agenda, take minutes, and establish a *parking lot* (a record of unfinished discussion items or new agenda items).
- *Respect members' contributions.* Make an effort to involve *all* participants which will move them from passive to active roles and improve decision making. Create ground rules and clarify norms about how members should interact. Pay attention to body language and address misunderstandings, disruptive behavior, or disagreements by reinforcing ground rules and refocusing the meeting.
- *Make sure everyone understands what's going on.* Frequently clarify and summarize what's happening to show consideration for participants and maintain focus. Help the group come to agreement; the facilitator should enter the discussion only when necessary. When action items arise from the discussion, assign a responsible person and due date for each. Revisit the *parking lot* and assign follow-up items, if needed.
- *Use time wisely.* Members should be polled to find the best times of the month, week, and day for them to meet. Set time limits

for agenda items, use a timekeeper and recorder, and keep the meeting moving. A meeting that runs more than two hours leads to frustration and fatigue.

- *End by summarizing decisions and assignments.* Review action items to end the meeting on a note of accomplishment. This summary and the meeting minutes will remind members about expected tasks after adjournment. Review the meeting process; ask the group what went well and what needs to be improved.

With a solid purpose, agenda, and commitment to involving meeting participants in planning, preparing for, and attending the meeting, your coalition will be known for running efficient, effective meetings (Mind Tools 2012). Use **TOOL 12: Coalition Meeting Checkup** to improve your next meeting.

TOOL 12: Coalition Meeting Checkup	Yes	No
✓ Members feel that our meetings are a good investment of their time.	☐	☐
✓ We usually stay on track during our meetings.	☐	☐
✓ Member participation is usually balanced.	☐	☐
✓ Our meetings are usually well facilitated.	☐	☐
✓ Meetings usually begin and end on time.	☐	☐
✓ Members share responsibility to ensure meetings are effective.	☐	☐
✓ We consistently accomplish meeting objectives.	☐	☐
✓ We regularly evaluate what is and isn't working.	☐	☐
✓ Our meetings are not interrupted by phones, people coming and going, etc.	☐	☐
✓ At meeting's end, members take responsibility for action items.	☐	☐

Create effective written documents. Another valuable way to communicate with coalition members and the wider community is to create minutes, annual reports, and community action plans that actually are read and followed. These documents should be clear and accurate since they become part of your coalition's historical record.

Meeting minutes. Minutes should be a record of what was *done*, not what was *said*. Readers should be able to visualize what occurred at the meeting. **TOOL 13: What Should Meeting Minutes Contain?** can serve as a guideline for effective meeting minutes (Rules On Line 2012).

TOOL 13: What Should Meeting Minutes Contain?
✓ Name and type of meeting—regular, annual, or special meeting ✓ Date, place, and time that the meeting began and ended ✓ Names of the facilitator/chair and recorder or their substitutes ✓ Names of voting members attending—was quorum reached? ✓ Names of guests and their subject matter ✓ Were minutes from previous meeting approved or corrected ✓ Motions made: Record exact wording of motion, motioner, seconder and results of vote ✓ Reports: Names of report, person presenting it, and action taken ✓ If report was written, attach it; oral reports may be summarized ✓ Other actions, assignments, deadlines, and recommendations ✓ Recorder's signature once minutes have been approved.

A tabular minutes format like the one in **TOOL 14: Meeting Minutes Template** is helpful for those who were unable to attend the meeting or as a reminder of responsibilities prior to the next meeting.

Other methods of communication. The best way to communicate with your members is in ways that they like best, so just ask them what they prefer. Even if they choose e-mail as the primary method, you should ask how often they want to hear from you (for example, once per week or per month). Internet-enabled social media can contribute to and improve every phase of your coalition's activities from assessing and planning to implementing to sharing documents and evaluating your strategies. "In 2013, social media and information sharing sites, such as Facebook, YouTube, and Twitter are among the most accessed websites on the internet with more than 1 billion, 800 million and 500 million users, respectively" (Bernhardt et al. 2013, 129). These media will enhance your coalition's ability to implement evidence-based change strategies in ways that are more efficient and effective than traditional communication methods. New media tools help:

- Engage diverse sectors of the community and connect them to your coalition and its partners for long periods of time
- Access and analyze community health data for planning and prioritizing your strategies
- Deliver personalized, relevant health messages to priority populations at appropriate times
- Collect and store process and outcome data for monitoring and evaluation purposes (Bernhardt et al. 2013, 130)

TOOL 14: Meeting Minutes Template			
Date			
Type of Meeting	❑ General ❑ Steering Committee ❑ Work Group		
Attendees			
Recorder	Name		
Topic	Discussion	Action or F/U	Who
1.	• Key discussion points • Decisions made	What, by when?	Responsible person(s)?
2.	• Key discussion points • Decisions made		
3.	• Key discussion points • Decisions made		
4.	• Key discussion points • Decisions made		
Announce-ments			
Adjourn	Next meeting time, date, location		

E-blasts and e-newsletters are effective, efficient methods to get information to members quickly. You also may decide to send out a monthly blog or use LinkedIn, Facebook, Twitter, Google Docs, Share-Point, Flickr or many other platforms to interact and share coalition videos, photos, and stories. Websites such as Go To Meeting can be used to connect partners to each other to hold online meetings with shared documents.

The key point is to be more accessible to members and visible to the greater community. Now that you have built the essential foundation of the coalition and established operating procedures, it's time to get to work, which will be covered in part III.

BUILD YOUR COALITION

RECAP

- True collaboration requires a commitment to shared goals, a jointly developed structure and shared responsibility; mutual authority; accountability for success; community assessment; and sharing of resources, risks, and rewards.
- To build an effective coalition, you should analyze the issue(s) on which the coalition will focus; create awareness of the issue(s); conduct initial planning and recruitment; develop resources; build infrastructure and leadership; and create an action plan that leads to policy, systems, and environmental changes in your community.
- Clear vision and mission statements generate coalition support and awareness, identify partners, reduce conflict, and minimize time costs and distractions from appropriate actions. The process of creating these tools may be as critical as the products themselves.
- A coalition's structure should fit its goals and resources and be no more complex than necessary. Form should follow function to ensure flexibility and responsiveness.
- Organizations are more likely to retain members when they have:
  - Positive social interactions
  - Access to information and resources
  - Recognition for their contributions
  - Influence in decision making
  - Useful orientation and training
  - Varied, fulfilling opportunities to participate
  - Outcomes from their efforts
- Diverse representation and engagement from businesses, local government, schools, and non-profit organizations help ensure that strategies are carried out effectively.
- A transformational leader is a change agent who creates and articulates a clear vision, empowers others to achieve at higher standards,

leads as a peer problem solver, and builds broad-based participation to transform the organization and/or community around him or her.

- A volunteer job description and commitment letter or MOU clarifies the expectations of each organizational partner.
- With a solid purpose, agenda, and commitment to involving participants in planning, preparing for, and attending meetings, your coalition will be known for running efficient, effective meetings.

Coalition Building Resources

BoardSource. This website offers practical tools, best practices, and training and leadership development for leaders of nonprofit organizations, including coalitions. It provides an extensive database, consultants, material on nonprofit governance, and a biennial international conference. http://www.boardsource.org/

Coalitions Work. This is a comprehensive coalition-building website that offers tools and other resources for building effective coalitions at the community level. Tools for every facet of coalition work are downloadable and free. Training, strategic planning, and problem solving for coalitions are available by consultation with Frances Butterfoss, founder and president. http://www.coalitionswork.com

Community Anti-Drug Coalitions of America (CADCA). CADCA's National Coalition Institute provides coalition training, technical assistance, evaluation, research, and capacity building. Its website has information on policy and advocacy, training materials (newsletters, Strategizers, primers, beyond the basics, and briefs) and interactive media. Materials focus on substance abuse, but are applicable for all community prevention efforts. http://cadca.org

Community Organizing and Community Building for Health and Welfare, **3rd Edition**, edited by Meredith Minkler, provides approaches community building/organizing from collaborating with communities on assessment and issue selection to using coalition building, media advocacy, and social media to enhance effectiveness. The appendices offer a variety of guidelines, exercises, and tools.

Community Tool Box. Work Group on Health Promotion and Community Development, University of Kansas. This website provides practical information to support coalition work in health and development. It features sections on all phases of coalition building that include descriptions of tasks, guidelines, examples, checklists of points to review, and training materials. The vast resources of the CTB are organized by what you may want to do: how-to guidance, toolkits, troubleshooting, and evidence-based practice. http://ctb.ku.edu/en/default.aspx

PART III
Make It Work!

MAKE YOUR CAMPFIRE WORK!

Lighting Your Fire

After the site preparation, fuel gathering, and laying the fire, it's finally time to ignite the fire!

1. Position yourself between the prevailing wind and fire lay.
2. Strike the match toward you while applying pressure to the match head with a finger. With your hand as a windbreak, hold the match at a 60-degree angle so the flame will burn up the match.
3. Hold the match in place and let it get going first, and then extend it into the tinder. You're on your way.
4. Light *under* the tinder and make sure kindling is above the tinder so the heat rises and burns.
5. Light *upwind* so the wind will blow fire into the fuel.
6. If necessary, blow gently at the base of the fire to get past the kindling stage.

If the fire ignites correctly, it should begin burning the kindling first, spread to your "cabin" within a few moments, and then, ignite the larger pieces of wood. You can encourage "wet" or hard-to-light fires by adding a few more pieces of kindling to the fire as it continues the ignition process.

MAKE YOUR COALITION WORK!

Now, your fledgling coalition is ready to roll up its proverbial sleeves and get to work. Just as the spark needs the right conditions to evolve into a steadily burning fire, your coalition needs the spark of an idea, the catalyst of a "fired up" advocate, or the recognition that a problem is growing in your community—a problem that needs a unified approach. In any case, it's wise to take one more check to be sure that the environment that surrounds your coalition is ready to accept the new ideas and changes that are about to be proposed. Such an assessment also will help your coalition learn about the resources and assets that your community has to offer.

Community Planning and Assessment

Community planning is a process of assessing the needs of your community and assessing the capacities or assets that are available to meet those needs. This assessment process helps you craft a clear picture of your community and can be the starting point for planning—developing awareness of critical issues, creating a shared vision, and promoting strategies for community change. The simpler the assessment and planning process, the more likely it is to succeed. There is no one right way to plan; the primary benefit of planning is often the process itself. Planning is a structured way of involving a number of people in thinking about the future, and this is often is chief value (Wolf 2012, 281).

The planning process begins by convening a group of community stakeholders to establish a vision and prioritize the issues that require change. A climate of enthusiasm toward planning must be cultivated within the coalition; without it, a planning process has little chance of success (Wolf 2012, 282). Issues, prioritized by the group, guide what information must be collected in order to make decisions that create change. Planning is critical for building consensus and buy-in for dealing with pressing health issues that affect priority populations or specific parts of the community. The National Resource Center website suggests that community planning helps the community:

- Understand its needs, why they exist, and why they should be addressed.
- Share how the needs affect the community's quality of life.
- Identify community strengths, weaknesses, and asset gaps.
- Create an inventory of resources that can be leveraged to improve quality of life.
- Access data to decide how to use available assets to address community needs.
- Obtain a baseline for measuring future outcomes.

Identify community needs and assets. A major goal of health planning is to conduct an assessment to develop an informed understanding of the needs that exist within a community and the effects on its members. The Community Tool Box website defines *community needs* as "the gap between what a situation is and what it should be". By examining these gaps, we find what is lacking and focus on improvement. Communities face many pressing health and social needs such as substandard housing, inadequate food supply, rising health care and insurance costs, poor access to quality health care, and increased prevalence of diseases. These needs affect small or large numbers of community members including families, individuals, youth, seniors, businesses, community organizations, and faith-based organizations. When more parts of a community are affected by a particular need, we are more likely to find support for addressing them.

Again, on the Community Tool Box website, *community assets* are defined as "those things that can be used to improve the quality of life". Assets may include organizations, people, partnerships, facilities, funding, regulations, policies, and a community's collective experience. Any positive aspect of the community is an asset that can be leveraged to develop effective solutions. A critical premise for beginning any health planning effort is that even the most under-resourced communities are asset rich.

An *assets-based approach* to community assessment is different from traditional approaches in that it recognizes community problems and challenges, but focuses on its assets and strengths. To use this approach, pose these four basic guiding questions to your stakeholders (Wolff 2012, 127):

1. What are the strengths of this community?
2. What issues is this community struggling with?
3. How can you be part of the solution and help in the community-building process?
4. What do you need from us, the coalition partners?

By appreciating the community's assets and challenges, we envision how the community environment can change and how we can ignite or encourage that change. This viewpoint will help us engage in activities that build supportive environments to help make the healthy choice, the easy choice for the community's residents.

Take Action: Develop a Community Action Plan

The National Resource Center website suggests six steps that coalitions can take to mobilize and engage their partners and stakeholders in a comprehensive community health planning process. These steps will help your coalition anticipate potential barriers and position itself for success. Each step is distinct, but information identified in one step may change your approach to another.

Action Step 1: Define the scope
Action Step 2: Collaborate
Action Step 3: Collect Data
Action Step 4: Determine key findings
Action Step 5: Set priorities and create an action plan
Action Step 6: Share Your Findings

Action Step 1: Define the scope. Your planning group may develop more than one vision of a healthy community and/or more than one way to accomplish it. Community issues are complex and interrelated. It's easy to expand the range of issues to include in your assessment beyond your capacity. To define the scope of your assessment, clearly identify the community issue, the affected community members, the geographic area, and key questions to answer. Focus on what you *need* to know versus what is *good* to know.

- What are the community demographics (income levels, races/ethnicities, and ages)?
- What are the faith- and community-based organizations that serve the community? What services do they provide and to whom?
- What services are local public agencies providing and to whom?
- What organizations are funded to address the community issues? What do residents see as the primary needs for this community?
- What strategies are being used to address the issue? Any positive outcomes?
- Who are the community leaders who are concerned with the issues we want to address?
- What community organizations focus on these issues and deliver services?
- Do partnering opportunities exist with other nonprofits or voluntary organizations?
- What are the gaps in community service? What would a complete system look like?

TOOL 15: Checklist for Choosing Coalition Issues may help you prioritize the issues that your community faces (Bobo, Kendall & Max 2001, 24-8).

TOOL 15: Checklist for Choosing Coalition Issues			
Use these questions to help your coalition choose its issue focus. For each potential issue, record a 1 for "yes" and a 0 for "no" answers. If an issue receives an "unsure" answer, then coalition members need to do further research in order to clarify the issue.			
Will the issue (or resolving the problem) ...			
	Yes	No	Unsure
1. Be consistent with community values and vision?			
2. Build community empowerment?			
3. Be winnable?			
4. Be widely felt?			
5. Be easy to communicate and understand?			
6. Provide opportunities for people to learn about and be involved in making decisions and policies?			
7. Build strong, lasting organizations?			
8. Have a clear, feasible time frame?			
9. Build leadership that is accountable?			
10. Result in real improvement in people's lives?			
11. Provide potential for developing resources or raising funds?			
12. Link local issues to regional, national and/or global issues?			

Action Step 2: Collaborate. Collaborate with community partners to conduct your assessment. Collaboration engages community members, increases access to data sources to answer key questions, makes more resources available to conduct the assessment, and establishes relationships that will be critical for leading actions identified in the findings.

To reduce conflict and clarify expectations, a memorandum of understanding (MOU) outlines the key responsibilities of your partners and ensures that they fully understand and commit to the efforts involved. Potential community partners include corporations, nonprofit and community organizations, foundations that provide grants to your community, universities, and government entities. Examine the available time, effort, and human resources from your staff, volunteers, consultants, and board members. Establishing collaborations increases the resources you can use to conduct a high-quality and useful assessment. Develop a work plan to assign roles, responsibilities, and time frames for major assessment activities.

Action Step 3: Collect data. Data gathering is a powerful process that informs action planning and priority setting, as well as strategic improvements and outcomes. As you begin to think about the steps necessary to ignite and create change, you may realize that your group doesn't have sufficient knowledge to make decisions about potential strategies. Instead of basing your judgments on selected "stories" or contradictory anecdotes, you need to find credible sources of information and/or develop your own data-collection tools. In any data-collection effort, set limits on how much data you will collect and analyze. Consider the amount of time you will need and available resources before selecting methods. Prioritize your data-collection needs according to what is essential to complete your community assessment. Document your data-collection efforts by listing the key questions that you identified in Action Step 1 and, then identify likely information sources.

Start data collection with *secondary data* that others have already collected. Begin with local data sources then broaden your search if needed. Focus on quality rather than quantity of data, so you can dedicate more time to other parts of the assessment. Some data may have associated financial costs for access. Sample secondary data sources may include:

- America's Health Rankings (ranks health disparities, and rates of obesity, tobacco use and diabetes by state): http://www.americashealthrankings.org/Rankings

- Hospital data on births, deaths, and discharge diagnoses: State or local hospital system data varies in availability and may be accessed via state health departments or contracting agencies. National Hospital Discharge Survey data is available from the CDC at http://www.cdc.gov/nchs/nhds/nhds_products.htm.
- Insurance claims data: Organizations and employers that meet certain qualifications can access patient-protected Medicare data from the Centers for Medicare and Medicaid Services (CMS) that combines private sector with Medicare claims data to identify which hospitals and doctors provide the highest quality, cost-effective care. Local/national insurance companies may provide disaggregated claims data to qualified organizations.
- Healthy People 2010 Data: National data from the CDC at http://www.cdc.gov/nchs/healthy_people/hp2010/DATA2010. htm. Other data on various topics are available from the CDC at http://www.cdc.gov/DataStatistics/.
- State-level data on chronic diseases: The American Diabetes, Heart, Cancer or Lung Associations and other advocacy groups' websites have links to state-level data.
- CARES Public Data: GIS data layers that have been added, updated, and maintained since the Center for Applied Research and Environmental Systems (CARES) launched its CARES Map Room in 2000. Access is easiest through the Community Commons website where you can create maps of your own community after registering. http://initiatives.communitycommons. org/tool/maps/Default.aspx.

Primary data is collected by the person or group conducting the assessment. Use this type of data collection to address questions that can't be answered using secondary sources or to better understand a particular issue. Collect primary data using surveys, observation, focus groups, interviews, and case studies. Your timeline should reflect the level of detail needed for your assessment. Clarify who will carry out different parts of the data-collection plan; set data-collection deadlines and stick to them.

Action Step 4: Determine key findings. This step will generate a lot of data about community needs and assets. Analyze it to identify your key findings, which help validate anecdotal evidence of community needs and assets, highlight significant trends found in the data collection process, reveal differences across community sectors, and clarify answers to the assessment's key questions. Analysis will help you summarize your data; it may include sorting, graphing, conducting statistical analyses, or simply identifying patterns. Examples of key findings might include:

- Strengths, gaps, opportunities, and challenges that are noted by many people or groups
- Programs or efforts that have produced significant results
- Increases, decreases, or changes in health status over time
- Changes in attitudes or behavior of people over time
- Environmental conditions that may affect the community's health
- Disparities in data among certain ethnic or racial groups, age or gender groups, or geographic sectors of the community

At this point, you will need to decide whether you need to collect further data or if you are ready to create an action plan.

Action Step 5: Set priorities and create an action plan. A community assessment enables you to make informed decisions about your goals and objectives and identify specific community needs. Priority setting based on your findings requires building consensus among groups with different opinions and views on how community issues should be addressed. Once priorities are determined, your action plan will identify specific actions and deadlines, as well as a persons and organizations responsible for each action. Use **TOOL 16: Coalition Action Plan** as a template for your action plan. For each part of your plan, decide how to measure effectiveness. Use measures that define your strategy and are tracked over time. Suggestions for setting priorities include:

- Providing key information prior to decision meetings.
- Nurturing relationships throughout the planning process.

IGNITE!

- Cultivating open communication—recognize the strength in differing viewpoints.
- Allowing time for people to reflect and digest information and modify decisions.
- Striving for consensus—emphasize what is at stake and why you are doing this.
- Resisting the urge to over analyze information or rush to meet deadlines.
- Building on existing strengths to ensure that you have a well-defined action plan.
- Ensuring that individuals responsible for carrying out tasks are committed to make change.

TOOL 16: Coalition Action Plan					
MISSION:					
GOAL 1:					
GOAL 2.					
Goal	Objectives	Major Strategies and Timelines	Defining Success (outcomes, by when?)	Partners	Resources
					Barriers
1					
2					

Logic Models. You may decide to create a logic model or a roadmap that describes the coalition's core elements and the connections between them. This helps you to describe the coalition's strategies and projected outcomes, which are essential for preparing evaluations, grant proposals, or sustainability plans. Creating a logic model will help you set goals and objectives for what "success" would look like. The University of

Wisconsin Cooperative Extension website and CDC Program Evaluation Guide are reliable resources for constructing logic models. Major logic model elements are:

- **Inputs/Resources**—materials that a coalition uses to reach desired results. Types of inputs are people's ideas and time, money, equipment, facilities, and supplies.
- **Strategies or Activities**—actions taken by coalition to produce desired results.
- **Outputs**—tangible outcomes of coalition strategies.
- **Outcomes**—short-term changes in knowledge, attitudes, understanding, perceptions, and behaviors; intermediate changes in behavior, skills, practices or capabilities; or long-term changes in health or social status, policies, systems, or environments.
- **External Influences**—positive or negative factors outside of your control that may influence coalition or strategy outcomes, such as geography, economy, or politics.

Logic Model

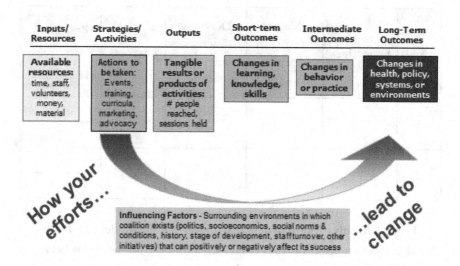

You may use **TOOL 17: Coalition Logic Model** to create your logic model.

TOOL 17: Coalition Logic Model					
Inputs	Activities/ strategies	Outputs	Short-term outcomes	Intermediate outcomes	Long-term outcomes

Action Step 6: Share the findings. The last step is to distribute your plan and share what you've learned. The community is more likely to support these efforts when people clearly understand what their community needs. Hold community meetings or summits to share the report or issue press releases to increase distribution to different media outlets. Use charts and graphs to illustrate your findings. Besides publishing the full report on partner websites, create a one-pager that summarizes key findings and actions that derive from community assets or needs. Continue to engage community members to build work groups and provide opportunities for community members who weren't involved in the assessment to carry out the plan.

Initiate Strategies
I am building a fire and every day I train,
I add more fuel.
At just the right moment, I light the match.
—Mia Hamm

Once your community assessment is finished and you have created your action plan, the next step is to develop and carry out strategies to achieve your goals. Effective strategies should reflect the values, mission, and priorities of the coalition and build on existing community resources, opportunities, and programs/services. Coalitions are usually judged on the merit of the activities and services that they provide within their communities. Some implement initiatives themselves, some sub-contract with organizations outside of the coalition to be "implementers," and others encourage and work with member organizations to carry out agreed-upon strategies. However your coalition decides to proceed, it is critical to get moving.

Strategies that change communities. Coalitions are ideally built to impact health and social issues at the community level. Instead of addressing problems at the level of individual behavior change, coalitions strive to change the policies, systems, and environments (PSE) that shape the choices that communities make. As community coalitions across the nation have discovered, it's really about making the healthy choice, the easy choice. The health impact pyramid shows the levels of impact of PSE strategies (CDC 2011, 57).

Health Impact Pyramid

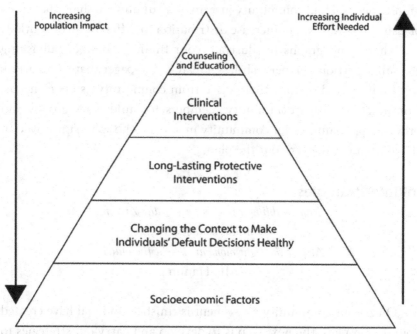

Frieden, T. R. Am J Public Health 2010;100:590-595

PSE strategies in the bottom tiers of the pyramid focus on improving socioeconomic factors and physical and social environments. These strategies have more impact than strategies in the top two tiers (educational or counseling programs or direct clinical services) for several reasons (Frieden 2010, 591).

- They benefit and impact more people/populations that are at risk for poor health.
- They can spread effectively throughout community settings, sectors, and levels (as the National School Lunch Program and tobacco-free policies have shown).
- They are more sustainable and can lead to significant cost savings. For example, it's estimated that if $10 per person per year were invested in community-based strategies to improve physical activity and nutrition, and prevent tobacco use, more than $16 billion would be saved in medical expenses per year within five years (Braveman and Egerter 2008, 43).

Experiences in tobacco taxes; school immunization laws; and vehicle safety, drunk driving, and seatbelt laws strengthen the case for implementing PSE change (CDC 2011, 58). Similarly, the National Community Anti-Drug Coalition Institute (CADCA) identified seven change strategies that, *when implemented together*, increase the likelihood of effectively reducing community level problems (CADCA 2009, 19):

Individual strategies
- Provide information through educational workshops or media.
- Enhance skills of participants, members, and staff/
- Provide support and encourage people to participate in activities that reduce risk or enhance protection/

Community and environmental strategies
- Enhance access or reduce barriers to increase the ease, ability, and opportunity to utilize systems and services.
- Change consequences by providing incentives or disincentives to increase protective behaviors of decrease risky behaviors.
- Change the physical design or structure of the environment to reduce risk or enhance protection.
- Modify or change policies, bylaws, rules, or laws.

The following graphic represents sample strategies recommended by the Community Anti-Drug Coalitions of America (2009, 19).

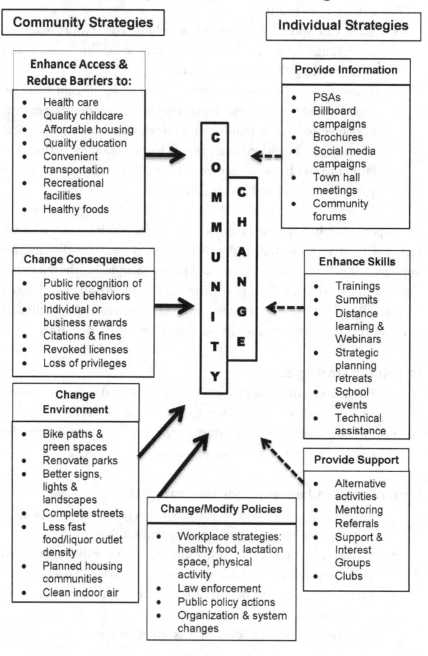

Community versus Individual Strategies

Community Strategies

Enhance Access & Reduce Barriers to:
- Health care
- Quality childcare
- Affordable housing
- Quality education
- Convenient transportation
- Recreational facilities
- Healthy foods

Change Consequences
- Public recognition of positive behaviors
- Individual or business rewards
- Citations & fines
- Revoked licenses
- Loss of privileges

Change Environment
- Bike paths & green spaces
- Renovate parks
- Better signs, lights & landscapes
- Complete streets
- Less fast food/liquor outlet density
- Planned housing communities
- Clean indoor air

COMMUNITY CHANGE

Change/Modify Policies
- Workplace strategies: healthy food, lactation space, physical activity
- Law enforcement
- Public policy actions
- Organization & system changes

Individual Strategies

Provide Information
- PSAs
- Billboard campaigns
- Brochures
- Social media campaigns
- Town hall meetings
- Community forums

Enhance Skills
- Trainings
- Summits
- Distance learning & Webinars
- Strategic planning retreats
- School events
- Technical assistance

Provide Support
- Alternative activities
- Mentoring
- Referrals
- Support & Interest Groups
- Clubs

Characteristics of successful strategies. Regardless of whether your strategies focus at the individual or community level, they will be more likely to achieve realistic goals and community support if they 1) use resources efficiently, 2) complement existing programs, 3) are culturally competent, 4) provide a focus for coalition member work efforts, 5) achieve intermediate outcomes, and 6) promote coalition credibility by addressing community issues in innovative ways (Foster-Fishman et al. 2001, 248). One way to find effective practices/strategies is to look those that work (Schorr 1997).

- Successful strategies are comprehensive, flexible, and responsive. They address many aspects of an issue and change according to the needs of participants and the community. They evolve over time and continually improve. When organizations adopt a new practice or idea, they often make it their own by changing it to meet their particular needs (Rogers 1995). These reinvented innovations work better, are more likely to be adopted, are more responsive to local conditions, and become "owned" by community members.

- Successful strategies are managed by competent, committed individuals with strong management and communication skills. Competent staff: 1) experiment, take risks, and seek evidence of results; 2) commit to build leadership and other community capacities; 3) provide quality service with support from the coalition and lead agency for ongoing education/training; and 4) build strong, collaborative relationships with community members based on mutual trust and respect.

- Successful strategies have reasonable costs that directly relate to expected benefits.

- Successful strategies involve staff, partners, and the community in planning, implementing, and decision making.

- Successful strategies build shared purpose among staff, partners, and participants to help overcome barriers and setbacks. Core values, such as a passion for the work and social justice, encourage personal development and empower participants to succeed.

Policymakers often seek "silver bullets" for solutions to social issues and want to fund *the* program that can eliminate *the* problem. However, poor community outcomes rarely result from a single incident or source; other supporting structures and institutions must work to strengthen the community as well. The best strategies serve as "community-building anchors" and create opportunities for community members to exercise leadership (Bruner 2004, 2).

Deciding which strategies to use. Strategies that are easier or most feasible often are those with the least evidence. Coalitions often jump into strategies, such as conducting health fairs or creating resource guides, even though these efforts have minimal impact on changing behavior or long-term outcomes. Start by asking whether justification for the potential strategy exists and whether it represents a best or promising practice. The Guide to Community Preventive Services (http://www.thecommunityguide.org/index.html) and the Roadmaps to Health presented by Country Health Rankings & Roadmaps (http://www.county-healthrankings.org/roadmaps/what-works-health/choosing-your-strategy) provide in-depth guidance to: 1) prioritize among possible strategies that you might use; 2) assess your community's available resources, political constraints, and readiness; and 3) determine whether a policy or program needs to be adapted to fit your community. The following evidence ratings can help you develop a "short list" of strategies to consider more comprehensively in your community (Roadmaps to Health):

- **Scientifically supported strategies**: Your top priority.
- **Some or mixed evidence strategies**: Use when those with stronger evidence aren't available or appropriate, and you have limited evaluation resources.
- **Expert opinion strategies**: Use when you have the time and resources to thoroughly assess effects.
- **Insufficient evidence strategies**: Use when you want to innovate, and have time and resources to fully assess effects.
- **Evidence of ineffective strategies**: Invest your resources elsewhere.

Prioritizing strategies. Strategies should be prioritized based on changes in external conditions, available funding, and your coalition's capacity for implementing them. After developing a list of potential strategies, evaluate and prioritize that list. The coalition should discard strategies that aren't relevant to its core set of goals. Consider the context of your community—the "fit" of the strategy along with the evidence of its effectiveness will help your coalition make strategic decisions about when to implement tried and true options and when to be more innovative. Involving other stakeholders, including local data and subject matter experts, can help answer these questions. For each potential strategy, use the criteria in **TOOL 18: Prioritizing Your Strategies** to evaluate its feasibility and likelihood of success (Butterfoss 2007, 398). After you apply these criteria, the list of potential strategies may be reduced to two or three that best fit the criteria. Then, these should be vetted with key coalition partners to decide if they are feasible and appropriate.

TOOL 18: Prioritizing Your Strategies

- ❑ Does justification for the strategy exist?
- ❑ Does the strategy represent a best or promising practice?
- ❑ Does the strategy reflect coalition goals and objectives?
- ❑ Is the strategy aligned with priorities of the lead agency, staff
- ❑ members and community partners?
- ❑ Is the strategy supported by resources of staff and partners who will carry it out?
- ❑ Does the strategy mesh with existing ones in the community?
- ❑ Is the strategy culturally appropriate for the priority population?
- ❑ What barriers may stand in the way of carrying out this strategy?
- ❑ Is the strategy cost effective?
- ❑ Is the strategy politically feasible?
- ❑ How will success be measured and evaluated?
- ❑ Is the strategy likely to have a positive impact, such as improving access to or delivery of services and maximizing resources and partners' efforts?

Finally, coalitions should research whether strategies that they plan to implement have been tried before and were effective. By focusing on proven and promising strategies, your coalition can benefit from others' experience of how to make it even more effective.

Carrying out your strategies. Strategies and activities can be piloted, phased in, or initiated all at once (McKenzie et al. 2005, 277-279). Pilot testing allows planners to "work out any bugs" before the activity is offered to more people in the priority population. The new strategy should be piloted in a similar setting with people like those who will eventually use it. The coalition should assure that the strategies are carried out and work as planned, resources are adequate, and participants evaluate the strategy. Once the strategy has been piloted and revised, the coalition should gradually phase it into control for quality and avoid being overwhelmed by a large number of participants. Phasing in can occur by gradually adding more parts of the initiative, limiting the number of participants, offering it in select locations, or offering it for different levels of ability, such as beginner, intermediate, and advanced (McKenzie et al. 2005, 279).

Total initiation should be used only for strategies such as screenings or trainings, where resources don't allow for trial runs. Note that the strategy or intervention may not be entirely new, but may be an adaptation of one that already exists or was used by another coalition in a different setting or for a different population. Paying attention to the following tasks will help ensure that implementation leads to positive outcomes (Fixsen et al. 2009, 533-4):

- Train and coach staff and volunteers who will implement the strategy, and evaluate their performance.
- Use social marketing and media techniques to make communities aware of the planned strategy.
- Use incentives and positive reinforcement to encourage participation in the initiative.
- Monitor strategies to assure that they are implemented as planned (i.e., with fidelity).
- Regularly evaluate whether strategies are working and adapt them as necessary.
- Provide administrative structures and processes to assure that ongoing resources and support are available.

The coalition must accomplish all of this in the context of changes in governments, leadership, funding levels, economic boom-bust cycles, and shifting of social priorities. Implementation of any new strategy almost always requires organizational change. In order for change to occur, a coalition must have these elements in place (Fixsen et al. 2005, 538):

- Leadership that is committed to implementation process
- Stakeholders who are involved in planning/selecting strategies and encouraging buy-in and ownership during implementation
- A team that oversees the implementation process
- Organizational structures and practices that are aligned to support planned strategies
- Resources that provide for costs, effort, equipment, manuals, materials, recruiting, access to expertise, and re-training for new roles associated with implementing an innovation
- Time for leadership development, coaching, planning, and evaluation

Working with your partners. Coalitions should engage in a variety of community service strategies, research activities, and advocacy actions in order to satisfy the diverse interests of coalition members. The mix of these strategies can vary at any given time, but effective coalitions learn how to juggle priorities to meet their members' needs, without concentrating on any one activity that alienates partners or is competitive. The primary role of coalitions is not to provide community services and programs—or else they risk competing with their partner organizations. Instead, create other roles for your coalition that stimulate long-lasting change, such as:

- Incubator of novel ideas and methods
- Vehicle for testing strategies that can be shared with partners if they work
- Advocate for the underserved or those experiencing disparities in health
- Linking pin that fosters new relationships among its partner organizations
- Trainer/technical assistance provider that builds skills and capacities of its members and the community

Encourage Commitment, Participation, and Sharing of Resources

Members who perceive more benefits than costs of participation are more likely to engage in voluntary associations and coalitions, and be satisfied and committed (Butterfoss and Kegler 2009, 258). Similarly, participation is fostered when members are committed to and have positive attitudes toward collaboration, the proposed project or priority issue, and their own and others' experience and capabilities (Foster-Fishman et al. 2001, 248–9). Pay attention to group dynamics because coalition members may share a history of conflict or have little experience of working in partnership with others (Bartunek et al. 1996, 715). Positive relationships can be fostered by creating a coalition climate that unites around a shared vision, shares decisions, resolves conflict, and addresses diversity in the coalition's plans (Foster-Fishman et al. 2001, 249). Positive relationships among members also are directly related to how much they participate, how satisfied they are with the work, and how well they put plans into action (Butterfoss and Kegler 2009, 256).

Member responsibilities. When recruiting members, we often use a soft-sell approach by saying, "It won't take much of your time—we just need someone to represent the housing authority." Then we wonder why that same recruit does not follow through as a member. It's much better to be clear about your expectations from the start and let the member know what his or her commitment will entail. **TOOL 10: Coalition Member Job Description**, in part II of this book, outlines the tasks, but you also might follow up with an informal checklist that is administered as part of a coalition discussion on commitment and responsibility. **TOOL 19: Am I a High-Functioning Coalition Member?** can be a springboard for a lively exchange among members.

Partner organization responsibilities. Often coalitions confuse the responsibilities of the *individuals* who represent the partner organizations that make up their membership with the responsibilities and commitment of the partner *organizations* themselves. It's fairly easy to miss this distinction because, after all, the representatives sit at your table and help carry out the strategies you adopt. These are the faces you see at meetings, the voices you hear on conference calls, and the written words you read in e-mails.

TOOL 19: Am I a High-Functioning Coalition Member?	Yes	No
1. I participate in determining the direction of the coalition.	❏	❏
2. I report coalition progress to my organization.	❏	❏
3. I share my organization's concerns/ideas with the coalition.	❏	❏
4. I am invested to develop ground rules for behavior in the coalition.	❏	❏
5. I share interests/concerns and assure that others are invited to do the same.	❏	❏
6. I listen and try to understand the views of others.	❏	❏
7. I assist in strategic planning and prioritize strategies into an action plan.	❏	❏
8. I help conduct a comprehensive community needs and asset assessment.	❏	❏
9. I help implement strategies, including those that involve my organization.	❏	❏
10. I serve as a resource for developing program activities.	❏	❏
11. I represent the coalition at key meetings and events.	❏	❏
12. I am a coalition ambassador and promote its mission widely.	❏	❏
13. I gather/relay appropriate information to coalition to guide decision making.	❏	❏
14. I prepare for and attend meetings on a regular basis.	❏	❏
15. I help develop resources to sustain the coalition.	❏	❏

These members are the *links* between their organization and your coalition. If they leave their jobs, move away, stop attending, or don't meet their responsibilities, the organizations that have committed to you have a responsibility to send new representatives. So, remember that, in most cases, the *organizations* that your members represent are the *actual coalition members*.

Members should regularly update the coalition about events, issues, and policy changes that occur in their organizations so that the coalition is responsive to those organizations as they deliberate issues and make decisions. Similarly, members should inform their organizations about key decisions that the coalition makes. For example, if the coalition decides to advocate a clean indoor air policy, the member should help promote it within his or her organization.

Minutes, reports, flyers, and e-mail alerts should regularly be distributed to members *and* their organizations. If a major decision is made by the coalition that has particular policy implications for an organization, coalition staff should confer directly with the organization's staff to ensure that critical information is communicated.

Sometimes, representatives of organizations are more committed to coalition goals and activities than are their organizations. Coalition staff should not assume that an organization is willing to commit resources or outward support based on the member's word. Some coalitions use annual *commitment letter*s to clarify members' roles, organizational intentions, and levels of support. These letters are geared toward organizational responsibility and help assure that the organization recognizes its commitment to the coalition. **TOOL 20: Model Commitment Letter** is an example of such a letter.

What to Do When Things Go Wrong

Sometimes, despite your best intentions, plans may go awry and problems may arise in your coalition or the surrounding community. This is to be expected, but not ignored. This book has provided you with practical tactics for preventing such problems, but **TOOL 21: What to Do When Things Go Wrong** offers common presenting symptoms, the problems they represent, and quick list of suggested solutions. These are by no means comprehensive, but use them to begin to get to crux of what might be wrong.

Each of these problems and its accompanying symptoms can be resolved if you and your coalition face it head on and try one or more of the suggested solutions. Of course, your coalition may rely on its own experiences and creativity to come up with novel approaches. There is no one right way to do this work.

Once your coalition is moving ahead strongly with its planned strategies, think seriously about how you will sustain its work over the long haul, which will be the focus of part IV.

TOOL 20: Model Commitment Letter

Our organization, *[name]*, is committed to be an active member of the *[name]* Coalition. We are dedicated to its vision, goals, and strategies that have been and/or will be decided by the Coalition. We are committed to the planning and collaboration that the Coalition will undertake. We acknowledge the contributions and expectations of other Coalition members. Benefits of membership include access to Coalition website and its resources, educational events, connection to other members and priority populations, and _____ *[list others that apply]*.

As general evidence of our commitment, we agree to do the following:
- ✓ Appoint representative(s) to attend Coalition meetings and activities
- ✓ Authorize representative(s) to make decisions on our behalf, except for decisions about _____ *[specify exceptions]*
- ✓ Read minutes/written materials to keep abreast of coalition decisions and activities
- ✓ Disseminate relevant information to organizational members or employees through electronic mailing lists, websites, and newsletters
- ✓ Keep Coalition informed of our organization's related activities

Our organization will commit the following resources to the Coalition:
- ✓ Access to our volunteers for Coalition tasks
- ✓ Financial commitment of $ _____ *[or dues, if appropriate]*
- ✓ In-kind contributions of staff time, material resources, meeting space, refreshments, and incentive items _____ *[Specify]*
- ✓ Connections to other organizations/individuals _____ *[Specify]*

Name of organization _____ Date _____
Signature of representative: _____

TOOL 21: What to Do When Things Go Wrong		
SYMPTOMS	**PROBLEM**	**SOLUTIONS**
• Failure to plan • Failure to act • Delays • Frustration	**Lack of focus or direction**	• Clarify vision, mission and goals • Develop action plan • Monitor progress
• History or past grievances surface • Unequal sharing of resources • Disruptive meetings • Hidden agendas • Lack of trust	**Turf battles and competition**	• Recommit to vision for community • Develop value statements • Prevent or openly address conflict • Promote face-to-face discussion to reveal partners' concerns/needs • Use informal conciliation • Use third-party mediation
• Member and leader burnout • Unreasonable demands on staff • New members fail to engage in work • Frustration • Resignations occur • Imbalance in power among organizations	**Unequal sharing of power, decision making and responsibility**	• Develop written roles and responsibilities for staff, leaders, and members • Create MOUs for member organizations • Meet with CEO/director of each organization yearly to clarify expectations • Review action steps at meeting's end and at start of next meeting • Hold annual coalition retreat to orient/train members on team building and delegation • Each organization gets one vote

TOOL 21: What to Do When Things Go Wrong		
SYMPTOMS	PROBLEM	SOLUTIONS
• Members are uniformed about meetings/events • Infighting erupts • Members and community don't see results from their efforts	Ineffective communication	• Promptly distribute minutes • Send monthly e-newsletters and items for partner newsletters • Develop/distribute 1-page organizational message • Hold annual state-of-the-coalition address to recap progress and future plans
• Dominance by professionals • Some community sectors aren't well represented • Coalition isn't respected or known in community • Community groups do not support coalition and its work	Poor links to the community	• Conduct gap analysis to build diverse representation • Engage in a serious recruitment campaign • Hold meetings and events in accessible, neutral sites • Speak about coalition opportunities at community events • Support activities of other community partners
• Ineffective work groups • Ineffective steering committee • Failure to develop, maintain or rotate leadership • Poor attendance • High "dropout' rate • Lack of ongoing training • Inadequate funding • Lack of results	Ineffective coalition structure or function	• Conduct strategic planning to realign mission and goals with structure and function • Build organizational chart • Conduct annual retreat and orientation for leaders • Institute 1- to 2-year leader term limits and annual elections • Commit to effective meetings and reporting • Have veteran leaders and members mentor new ones • Develop resource development or steering committee to develop budget, resources and funds

TOOL 21: What to Do When Things Go Wrong		
SYMPTOMS	**PROBLEM**	**SOLUTIONS**
• Poor or inconsistent attendance • Lack of follow through on tasks	**Time and loyalty conflicts**	• Use surveys and discussions to find best meeting times and fit between talents and tasks • Conduct annual review of commitment letters • Ask organization to send new representative with more time to offer coalition • Follow-up by chairs of non-attenders and those who fail to finish tasks
• Coalition is not recognized by media or key community leaders • Coalition doesn't receive grants or funding from proposals • Recruiting members and leaders is difficult • Expected outcomes don't occur • Community problems are unresolved	**Lack of outcomes**	• Develop logic model, action plan and evaluation plan • Collect data and consistently monitor short-term, intermediate, and long-term outcomes to hold partners accountable and help align efforts • Coordinate each partners' activities via an agreed-upon action plan • Use 1-page organizational message and social media to broadcast successes to current and prospective members and leaders • Contact foundations and funders to explore funding opportunities

RECAP

- The assessment process helps you craft a clear picture of your community and can be the starting point for planning—developing awareness of critical issues, creating a shared vision, and promoting strategies for community change.
- Health planning is critical for building consensus and buy-in for dealing with pressing health issues that affect priority populations or specific parts of the community.
- Collect just enough data to answer the key questions that have been developed by your community and coalition.
- Priority setting based on your assessment findings requires consensus building among community groups with various views and opinions about how issues should be addressed.
- Once priorities are determined, your action plan will identify specific actions and deadlines, as well as a person/organization responsible for each action.
- Effective strategies should reflect the values and priorities of the coalition and build on existing community resources, opportunities, and programs/services.
- Effective coalitions learn how to juggle priorities to meet their members' needs without concentrating on any one activity that alienates them or competes with their organizations.
- Positive relationships among members are directly related to how much they participate, how satisfied they are with the work, and how well they put plans into action.
- To reduce conflict and clarify expectations, memoranda of understanding (MOUs) or commitment letters outline your partners' responsibilities and ensure that they are committed to the efforts involved.

Community Assessment, Planning, and Implementation Resources

America's Health Rankings. This website ranks health disparities, and rates of obesity, tobacco use, and diabetes by state. You can see how all states rank on a given measure, view data by year, or compare states. This method balances how factors such as smoking, obesity, sedentary lifestyle, binge drinking, high school graduation rates, children in poverty, access to care, and incidence of preventable disease, contribute to a state's health. The tool is based on data from the US Departments of Health and Human Services, Commerce, Education, Justice and Labor; the US Environmental Protection Agency; US Census Bureau; American Medical Association; Dartmouth Atlas Project; and Trust for America's Health. http://www.americashealthrankings.org/Rankings.

University of Wisconsin Population Health Institute. Madison, Wisconsin. **County Health Rankings and Roadmaps.** The Rankings are based on a model of population health that emphasizes the factors that can help make communities healthier places to live, learn, work, and play. The Rankings illustrate *what we know* when it comes to what's making people sick or healthy. The Roadmaps show *what we can do* to create healthier places to live, learn, work and play.
http://www.countyhealthrankings.org/

University of Wisconsin Population Health Institute. Madison, Wisconsin. **What Works for Health.** This online tool identifies effective policies/programs to improve factors that affect health. Each program is given an evidence rating; the highest-rated programs/policies have been shown to work. Choose a health factor of interest (i.e., access to healthcare, tobacco use, employment, or environmental quality) and search evidence ratings for programs, policies, or system changes that address that health factor.
http://www.countyhealthrankings.org/what-works-for-health

Campbell Collaboration (C2). This website offers systematic reviews of interventions in areas such as crime, social welfare, and education.

Its Resource Center provides policy makers, researchers, and others with resources in training, research, knowledge translation, evidence-based decisions/practice, policy documents, guidelines, links, and tutorials. http://www.campbellcollaboration.org/resources/resource_center.php

Canadian Best Practices Portal for Health Promotion and Chronic Disease Prevention. This website provides decision makers with a comprehensive resource on best practices for chronic disease prevention/ control, and creates awareness of overall Canadian Best Practices System through communication and marketing activities for key audiences. http://cbpp-pcpe.phac-aspc.gc.ca/

Centers for Disease Control and Prevention, Atlanta, Georgia. **Strategic Alliance for Health (SAH) Implementation Guides.** SAH communities help 1) change policies, systems, and environments to promote physical activity and nutrition and reduce tobacco use/exposure; 2) improve/ increase access to quality health care; 3) eliminate health disparities; and 4) reduce complications/incidence of chronic disease. The fourteen guides help communities replicate strategies across sectors and chronic disease risk factors. Each offers lessons learned as well as guidance for planning, evaluating, and sustaining strategies. http://www.cdc.gov/healthycommunitiesprogram/communities/sah/index.htm#guides

Cochrane Collaboration. This website provides quality-assessed review evidence on diagnostic tests, health technology assessments, economic evaluations, and methods studies from the world's medical literature. It reviews standards for healthcare interventions/treatments and offers training and other services. Healthcare evidence is available in Spanish. The Cochrane Library (by subscription) contains Cochrane Reviews and other databases of reviews and controlled trials. http://www.cochrane.org/about-us/evidence-based-health-care/webliography

Community Commons. This healthy communities' movement website offers access to: 1) GIS data at state, county, zip code, block group, tract, and point-levels; 2) mapping, visualization, analytic, impact, and communication tools; 3) profiles and video narratives of collaboratives that are funded by philanthropy and government to build healthy, sustainable, livable, and equitable communities; and 4) peer forums to explore similar interests/challenges hosted by national technical assistance providers. http://www.communitycommons.org

Community Development. Data Information and Analysis Laboratory (CD-DIAL). (2001). Preparing for a Collaborative Community Assessment. Ames, IA: Iowa State University Extension. This university extension service offers practical, how-to education based on powerful university research. This publication covers why a community assessment should be conducted, the characteristics of successful community assessments, the steps involved in conducting them, and what to do after the assessment is completed. www.extension.iastate.edu/Publications/CRD334.pdf

Centers for Disease Control and Prevention. Atlanta, Georgia. **Guide to Community Preventive Services (Community Guide).** A resource to help you choose strategies/policies to improve community health/prevent disease. With oversight from the Community Preventive Services Task Force, the guide reviews scientific literature and makes recommendations by collaborating with government, academic, policy, and practice partners. It answers questions about what strategies have/have not worked, in which populations and settings, at what cost, benefits, and harms. http://www.thecommunityguide.org/index.html

Healthy People 2020 Structured Evidence Queries. This website makes evidence-based strategies related to Healthy People 2020 objectives easier to find. The National Library of Medicine has created one-click strategies to search *PubMed*, a database that provides access to citations from MEDLINE and other journals. http://phpartners.org/hp2020/index.html

Model Practice Database. The National Association of County and City Health Officials (NACCHO) created this guide for searching promising practices by keyword, state, type, or year. https://eweb.naccho.org/eweb/DynamicPage.aspx?site=naccho&webcode=mpsearch

Morrison, E. (2010). **Strategic Doing: The Art and Practice of Strategic Action.** West Lafayette: Purdue Center for Regional Development. This publication defines and describes the steps of "strategic doing", a set of principles, practices and disciplines for implementing strategy in a network or collaborative. It also focuses on developing new civic spaces; leveraging the collaborative power of Web 2.0; and building regional leadership. http://www.pcrd.purdue.edu/What_We_Do/SD/wp.pdf

National Business Coalition on Health. (2012). **Technical Action Guide: Community Health Planning.** This guide summarizes planning approaches/methods used by coalition grantees and explains how they mobilized/engaged community stakeholders. It provides lessons learned and recommendations for other coalitions to replicate consensus building to improve health outcomes.
www.nbch.org/nbch/files/ccLibraryFiles/ … /NBCH_TAG_F.pdf

Pew Partnership for Civic Change. **Solutions for America; The Guide for Civic Problem Solving.** This guide summarizes effective evidence-based strategies in addressing healthy communities and families, thriving neighborhoods, living-wage jobs, and viable economies.
http://www.solutionsforamerica.org/

Rotary International. (2008). **Community Assessment Tools: Companion Piece to Communities in Action - Guide to Effective Service Projects.** Evanston, Illinois. This guide provides information on using surveys, calendars, asset inventories, mapping, and focus groups to assess communities. www.rotary.org/RIdocuments/en_pdf/605c_en.pdf.

Underage Drinking Enforcement Training Center. (2012). **Community-based Programs: Survey and Community Assessment Tools.** This site contains sample assessment tools for communities and coalitions that need to gather information and data. It includes checklists, assessments, exercises and survey instruments.
http://www.udetc.org/surveyandcommunity.asp

Wisconsin Cooperative Extension Website. The site provides materials/examples to help community-based practitioners design, implement, and evaluate their programs. This link will help you create logic models for your strategies.
http://www.uwex.edu/ces/pdande/evaluation/evallogicmodel.html

PART IV
Sustain It!

SUSTAIN YOUR CAMPFIRE

Keeping Your Fire Going

Fuel wood is the life of the campfire. As you feed fuel to the bed of coals, the fire will continue to live. Remember that oak and maple hardwoods burn hot and long, while pine burns fast with more soot.

1. Keep a bucketful of water near your campfire for safety reasons.
2. Start burning smaller pieces of wood one end and work your way up to logs.
3. Collect more wood as you think you'll need it, or the fire will go out while you're looking for more.
4. Don't overbuild or add too much wood at once. Campfires can easily get away from you. Keep your campfire well within the borders of your fire pit and keep it small to avoid sparking.
5. You can breathe new life into a fire that has died down by stoking the coals and adding kindling and small pieces of wood.

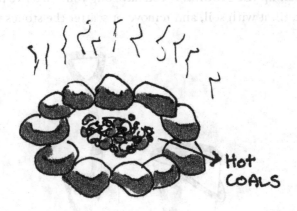

Hot COALS

Putting Out Your Fire

1. **Start early.** Putting out a fire completely takes longer than you think. Plan when you're going to bed or leaving and start putting out your fire about twenty minutes before then.

2. **Douse with water.** Your bucket of water will serve as your fire extinguisher. Avoid the impulse to pour all the water on the fire at once and flood the pit; someone else will need to use it later. Just use as much water as you need to put out the embers and charcoal. If you don't have water, mix dirt with the embers and stir until all material is cool. Don't bury the fire as it will smolder and could catch roots on fire that will eventually get to the surface and start a wildfire.

3. **Dredge and dig.** Stir the embers with a stick or shovel to ensure that all ashes get wet. When you don't see any steam or hear hissing noises, you're close to a completely extinguished fire.

4. **Touch test.** Put the back of your hand near the ashes. If you feel heat, it's too hot to leave. Keep adding water and stirring. As soon as it feels cool, you're good to go.

5. **Dispose the ashes.** Don't leave the next camper with a fire bed full of old ashes. If you made your own fire pit, leave the site the same way you found it. Never put fire ash into trashcans. Scoop up the cold ashes and spread them out around the campsite.

6. **Patch up the ground.** If you have dug your own fire pit, clean it out, fill it with soil, and remove or scatter the stones you used.

SUSTAIN YOUR COALITION!

It takes diligent effort to gather enough dry, quality wood and feed it continuously to your campfire to keep it burning through the cool evening. The campsite may be popular, and most of the downed wood has been gathered. The available wood may be damp, and the wind may not cooperate with your efforts to stir up the coals. Or maybe a light drizzle or fog sets in. So it goes with your collaborative efforts. You will face many challenges in keeping the fire burning under your community. Everything that you've read about up to now is actually the easiest part of any collaborative effort. The hardest part of any community initiative is not getting it started, but keeping it going long enough to achieve its goals.

What Is Sustainability?

Given the scarcity of resources and greater competition for funding, your community needs to maintain its capacity to work in partnership on its priority issues, so that the strategies they put in place will have lasting, or *sustainable*, impact. The Centers for Disease Control has created *The Sustainability Guide for Healthy Communities* that outlines the steps to sustainability with excellent examples from communities similar to yours (Bataan et al. 2011). In the guide, sustainability is defined as a community's "ongoing capacity and resolve to work together to establish, advance, and maintain effective strategies that continuously improve health and quality of life for all."

This working definition lets us know that sustainability isn't just about funding. It's about building the momentum to maintain community-wide change by maximizing your community's assets and resources. It's about ensuring that positive policies and practices become ingrained in the culture of your community and its organizations. It's about engaging key stakeholders to nurture long-term community support for your coalition's efforts.

To flourish in the long run, any organization needs to adapt to changes in needs and priorities, funding, leadership, and the economy. It also needs to effectively monitor the results of the policies it implements and modify those strategies accordingly. In order for sustainability to become a reality, then, coalitions need (Mosaica 2005):

- **Involvement in significant community activities.** The coalition is engaged in activities that address long-term community concerns and is considered worthy of continuing support. Procedures for monitoring, enforcing, and modifying PSE strategies are in place.
- **Strategic capacity.** The coalition is effective and demonstrates positive outcomes that justify its existence. Member organizations collaborate to provide high quality initiatives or services.
- **Clear values or operating principles.** The coalition is guided by shared values that are reflected in its priorities, strategies, and day-to-day operations.
- **Core leadership with strong commitment.** The coalition has a succession plan for leaders who are committed to the coalition, keep it focused, resolve conflicts, and carry out its work.
- **Diverse membership.** The coalition engages diverse sectors and community members including policymakers, businesses, residents, consumers, and beneficiaries.
- **Management capacity.** The coalition has sound financial and program management policies and procedures and staff/leaders who consistently implement them.
- **Community buy-in and support.** The coalition has individual and organizational members who value and support its work and speak on its behalf.
- **Power and influence.** The coalition is respected by key decision makers and credible because of its values, members, and work, enabling it to influence others.

To ensure that your coalition is sustainable for the long haul, it must focus on several key issues, which will be covered here in depth:

- Identify financial/in-kind support to maintain strategies long enough to achieve outcomes.
- Sustain energy and interest in the work.
- Spin off strategies and change structure or processes if needed.
- Evaluate coalition efforts.
- Expand or end collaboration when goals are reached.

Identify Resources to Sustain Strategies

One of the chief issues that coalitions face is how to support the organization and its activities in the years to come. Pay attention to the following four hallmarks of a fiscally sound non-profit organization and your coalition will face the future with confidence.

1. **Diversity in funding sources.** The coalition is not dependent for its survival on any single type or source of funding. Diverse funding reduces the imbalance in power that occurs when a single funder is controlling the coalition's budget. With multiple funding sources, the coalition can ensure that it is fulfilling its own goals, as well as funders' requirements. Funding should be flexible enough to support the core activities of the coalition— rather than earmarked for specific activities that are carried out by the collaborative. A budget of at least $25,000/year and funding from at least three different organizations are recommended (Leviton et al. 2006, 203). The coalition may obtain funds from a variety of sources: in-kind contributions from members, government agencies, foundations, corporations or small businesses; individual contributions; educational offerings; dues; community fundraising events; and fees for service.

2. **Internal generation of funds.** The coalition does not totally depend on external donations or grants, but receives significant in-kind support from its lead agency, partner organizations, and/ or other sources.

3. **Multi-year funding.** The coalition has some multi-year grants or contracts and does not have to raise the full amount of its budget each year.

4. **A community home and/or fiscal agent.** The coalition has a stable base of operations, or a "community home," and/or fiscal agent to position its efforts in the community and help ensure that essential functions continue, even in the face of internal or external change. A community home could be located within an existing business, government branch, community health organization, hospital, or foundation. The community home is a neutral broker of resources and has the infrastructure and capacity to: 1) solicit and accept a variety of funding sources, 2) appeal to a variety of community-based organizations, 3) manage competing interests, and 4) shift priorities according to changes in community needs and coalition goals.

501 c 3 non-profit status. A coalition may not have its own legal nonprofit status; instead, a partner agency or community home acts as the legal entity/fiscal agent. However, at some point, your coalition may decide to become a 501(c) 3 organization. Before doing so, consider the potential benefits and consequences. On the plus side, your coalition will become more independent and no longer be under the control of another agency. Thus, you can decide which resources to seek and apply for funds directly. Potential downsides are that: 1) the time and effort spent managing the coalition may detract from its strategies, and 2) your coalition actually may compete for funding with its own member organizations. These issues can be overcome with proper planning and bylaws, but you will need key partners to support this funding strategy.

Securing funding. After deciding what strategies your coalition will continue, think creatively about developing resources and leveraging funding sources. Continuing an effort does not necessarily mean continuing it in the same way. Leaders and members should analyze the coalition's current financial situation, including all funding sources and their timeframes. Be clear about which efforts you want to maintain and in what form, without focusing solely on monetary aspects. For example, you might eliminate an existing activity or program and replace it with a new strategy, or simply improve the efficiency with which you provide a service or product. Gifts-in-kind from members can be used to obtain needed equipment, supplies, software, and other items; pro bono labor/expertise can be recruited from your members and their contacts. Identify major and potential supporters of your efforts, gaps in funding, and where to reallocate existing resources. Consider different financial strategies that best fit with your coalition efforts. Think about striking a balance between the time and resources it takes to secure new funding and to implement existing activities. Look within your community to obtain financial resources—coalition members, an organization's board of directors, businesses, local foundations, public entities, and other community members. You may decide to create a resource development committee, hire a fund developer or outside consultant, or engage in marketing and public relations efforts (Marek et al. 2009, 7). Discussions from the decision-making process can be translated into a case for support for an effort. When deciding who might continue to fund an effort, discuss who benefits from your coalition's success and how to get them to help continue the effort.

Grants and other sources of funding. Grants have become one of the go-to sources for nonprofits that need to fund a strategy. Grant seeking can be a very time consuming process, so it's crucial that you absolutely need a grant before you look for one. You may even ask to join another organization's grant proposal as a sub-grantee or subcontractor. Besides grants, here are nine ideas to consider when looking for sustainable funding sources (Silver 2012, 10-12):

1. **Use fees to continue community improvements.** For example, charge fees to rent local park facilities to fund continuing after-school recreation activities.
2. **Leverage existing funding sources with local efforts.** For example, ask school districts or city and county governments to financially support community gardens, farmers' markets, and other efforts that fall within their own programs. Partner with the local parks and recreation department to monitor trail usage on a quarterly basis by sharing positions and resources.
3. **Request funding from local businesses and foundations.** For example, co-market programs with local businesses to create income. Before approaching local funders, plan how to support them to create a win-win situation.

4. **Ask coalition partners to add collaborative support costs to their funding proposals.**

5. **Become a line item in your fiscal agent or community home's budget. Hold one-time or continuing fundraising events.** Sponsor golf tournaments, recognition dinners, and fun runs/walks to raise revenues and community support at the same time. Take care that the event itself does not sidetrack the coalition from its mission and goals.

6. **Launch a fundraising campaign**—start with your members.

7. **Identify and secure a major contributor or sponsor.**

8. **Create a dues structure for coalition members.** Dues may provide financial security to cover gaps in funding. Ensure that members receive tangible benefits for their investment, such as educational opportunities, information sharing, recognition, strategic results, and relationships and links with other members.

9. **Charge fees for coalition services and products.** Create tools, resources, and educational materials to generate income for the coalition's other initiatives. Holding local conferences and educational events will provide continuing education for your community and coalition members. Make sure that the costs are reasonable and resources and events are high quality.

Market Your Coalition and Its Work

Early on, you developed your coalition's brand—its mission, byline, and logo. Like any for-profit organization, a coalition has a brand and a product to "sell." That product may be community health and well-being, equity, or social justice. Just like for-profit organizations, your coalition must decide how it will "get the message out" about its mission and goals. *Marketing* is the process by which an organization presents itself as valuable so that other organizations or individuals are willing to make an exchange in order to be part of that organization (Dowling et al. 2000, 42). Marketing may be used to help a coalition build a positive image, recruit members, or attract funders. Social marketing is a specific marketing technique that "harnesses audience participation to deliver value and specific behavioral goals for a social good" (Bernhardt et al. 2012,

131). A coalition may use social marketing techniques to help people and organizations change behaviors, policies, systems, and environments to promote health and well-being.

Coalitions have fewer resources than for-profit organizations for marketing themselves and their work. However, coalitions still can reach wide audiences through their promotions; they just have to manage budgets wisely when choosing which marketing techniques to use. The following list will help you get started with social media and marketing ideas to promote your coalition and its work (Wolf 2012, 156-61:

- ✓ Develop a website.
- ✓ Send out e-newsletters and e-blasts.
- ✓ Communicate via blogs and social media sites.
- ✓ Use direct mail to find new customers or donors.
- ✓ Send out news releases to media agents and key people on your mailing list.
- ✓ Hold occasional public relations events, such as community forums.
- ✓ Develop displays for high-traffic sites such as malls, community centers, and worksites.
- ✓ Convene community leaders in problem-solving meetings around issues of interest.

Develop an organizational message. One essential tool for "marketing" the coalition to potential funders, volunteers, and other supporters is a consistent, effective "organizational message" that communicates the coalition's unique purpose, scope of activities, and priority population. The organizational message should communicate what the coalition is, what it does, and why it is a vital force in the community. It should generate excitement and encourage the reader to learn more about your coalition. This message is less than one page long and consolidates your coalition's vision, mission, goals, and strategies. It may be used to recruit community members and introduce the coalition to potential partners, or may be included with requests for funding or for media coverage. The organizational message should (Mosaica 2005, 1-3):

- Clearly describe the coalition's purpose or mission—why it exists and its long-term goal.
- Provide history about the coalition's legal status or affiliation. Is it an independent nonprofit organization with its own tax-exempt status or under the non-profit umbrella of another organization? Who initiated the coalition? How and when was it initiated?
- Identify the coalition's service area. Does it serve a certain geographic area (e.g., neighborhood, zip code, section of city, town or county)?
- Identify the priority population served by the coalition. Does it focus on a particular group or subgroup (e.g., people with HIV/AIDS, refugee and immigrant families, children or youth of a particular age, women, and persons from a particular racial/ethnic group)?
- Describe its scope of activities or strategic focus. Does it provide direct services, training, advocacy, public education, and/or some other function? Does it focus on a particular program area, such as asthma, violence prevention, affordable housing, women's issues, or primary health care?
- Describe what is unique or compelling about the coalition. Is it is the only one of its kind, the only one using a certain approach, or the only one in the community?
- Effectively communicate its message. Be specific and avoid clichés, vague terms, jargon, or acronyms. Use active verbs and short sentences.
- Provide summary statistics and historical facts. Put the message in the context of what the community values.
- Tailor the message and wording for priority audiences. Emphasize different aspects of the coalition when seeking support for a particular strategy.

Sustain Energy and Interest in the Work

If you're through changing, you're through.
—Martha Stewart

To flourish in the long run, your coalition needs to be able to adapt to changes in needs and priorities, funding, leadership, and the economy. At the same time, it needs to effectively monitor the results of the strategies it implements and modify them as needed. To help sustain and make the best use of your coalition's resources, develop a sustainability plan that will enable it to diversify or expand the scope of its goals, membership, strategies, and funds.

Successful long-term planning depends on having a clear picture of a long-term mission and vision that includes aspects of your coalition's structure or strategies that should be maintained or improved (Lasker and Weiss 2003, 23). Consider the following suggestions:

- ✓ Create a shared understanding of what sustainability means to your coalition and other key stakeholders—agree that planning for sustainability is valuable
- ✓ Determine what type of structure and communication strategies will best suit coalition needs for the long run.
- ✓ Review, or expand, your mission and vision, goals, resource development, and timeline.
- ✓ Be clear about what sustainability means in the context of your strategies and activities.
- ✓ Involve more community leaders and partners in the sustainability-planning process.

If your coalition is ready to create a formal plan, follow the 10-step Sustainability Planning Process developed by the Center for Civic Partnerships (see references):

1. Create a shared understanding of sustainability.
2. Create a plan to work through the process.
3. Position your effort to increase your sustainability odds.
4. Look at the current picture and pending items.
5. Develop criteria to help determine what to continue.
6. Decide what to continue and prioritize.
7. Create options for maintaining your priority efforts.
8. Develop a sustainability plan.
9. Implement your sustainability plan.
10. Evaluate your outcomes and revise as needed.

One benefit of completing this process is that you will develop a Sustainability Plan, which your coalition can use to guide its future development. **TOOL 22: Sustainability Plan Outline** provides a template for your plan (Center for Civic Partnerships 2010).

TOOL 22: Sustainability Plan Outline

I. **Executive summary**
 - ☐ Organizational and/or program history (brief)
 - ☐ Definition of sustainability
 - ☐ Description of who was involved
 - ☐ Summary of efforts for which sustainability is an issue
 - ☐ Goals, needs, and costs for efforts being continued

II. **Situational analysis**
 - ☐ Organizational strengths as they relate to positioning
 - ☐ Current picture/pending items

III. **Criteria to determine program value-added benefits**
 - ☐ Identify what elements will be used to determine criteria (e.g., population reached, evidence of effectiveness, broad support)

IV. **Sustainability planning goal(s)**
 - ☐ Efforts to continue
 - ☐ Efforts to revise and continue
 - ☐ Efforts to ask another organization to continue

V. **Sustainability strategies**
 - ☐ Describe any organizational or structure changes
 - ☐ Recruit program champions and partners
 - ☐ Marketing and public relations
 - ☐ Funding
 - ☐ Communication of justification matrix

VI. **Action plan by strategy**
 - ☐ Develop SMART objectives (Specific, Measurable, Achievable, Relevant, Time-oriented) for organizational and policy efforts
 - ☐ Develop action plan and timetable for strategies

Build Coalition Members' Skills. Coalition members want to learn new skills, develop their capabilities, and grow their knowledge and careers. Helping them do so not only benefits the coalition as a whole, but it also helps motivate members to sustain their participation. Coalitions should support learning and training through workshops, one-on-one training, or other means. Training not only provides long-term benefits to your coalition members, but it also helps to sustain the efforts of the coalition itself. Training generally covers topics of collaboration and relevant health and social issues. To identify training priorities, your coalition might survey your members to assess training needs or consult with your coalition staff/leaders for recommendations.

Spin Off Strategies and Change Structure or Processes

Let's assume that one or more of your coalition's initiatives have really taken off. If you believe in the work you are doing, you'll want to keep it going when funding ends, politics change, or when staff or leadership changes occur in your coalition. The active process of establishing your initiative within your coalition, a partner organization, or the community is called *institutionalization* or *sustainability*. It involves not merely continuing your strategy or activity, but building relationships, practices, and procedures that become a lasting part of the community. Developing a plan for sustaining your initiative will increase its impact.

Planning for sustainability is more comprehensive and long term than much of the other planning you will do. It demands that you step away from the daily details of running your coalition and look at the whole picture. The Community Tool Box website proposes seven questions that are essential to ask when planning a sustainable effort. Ask your coalition's leaders to answer them first; then, pose them to partners as is practical:

1. What are the goals of our initiative?
2. What are the outcomes of our initiative?
3. What publicity has our initiative received?
4. How is our initiative structured and managed?
5. Does our initiative have sufficient staffing?
6. Is our budget sufficient to cover the initiative's expected and future costs?
7. What are some obstacles we may encounter, and how do we overcome them?

Once you have answered these questions, your course of action in dealing with your coalition's activities and strategies should be clearer. In essence, sustain the strategies that fit your mission, goals, staff and volunteer capacity, and financial ability. Those strategies that will be difficult to sustain should be discontinued or "spun off" to other partners or community organizations that are better suited and ready to "take them on." You can assist in the transition process by sharing your successes and lessons learned in implementing these strategies. Also, be sure to pass along any written records, tools, or associated products that will help the new organization to be empowered and successful in this endeavor. In this way, your coalition can serve as a mentor and technical guide for the organization that adopts your strategy.

In addition to spinning off strategies, your coalition may have to alter its structure or the way it does business in order to implement its strategies well and achieve its goals. Creating a new work group to manage a specific activity or program, seeking additional funding, hiring support staff, or recruiting new partners are all ways that a coalition can respond to changing demands or a new imperative. Because a coalition is, by its very nature, a dynamic organization, it can make these changes rather seamlessly as long as its membership and leadership are responsive and willing.

Use Evaluation to Sustain Your Coalition and Its Efforts

Monitoring and evaluating help ensure that resources are used wisely, goals and objectives are reached, and strategic improvements are made where needed.

- Monitoring is the process of collecting information to describe an initiative, answering questions such as, What? How much? How many?
- Evaluating, through in-depth analysis and comparisons, uses information gained through monitoring to identify ways to improve your coalition and its strategies. Evaluation addresses questions such as, Was the strategy effective? Did the strategy achieve its intended outcomes? Is one strategy more effective than another?

Evaluation can help you decide whether the current coalition structure serves its purpose, whether strategies were implemented well, and what outcomes occurred as a result. Evaluation can help your coalition improve its strategies over time, engage stakeholders, be more accountable to funders, and sustain itself. Keep these tips in mind throughout the planning process:

✓ Develop a logic model that shows how continuing strategies will help improve community outcomes. (Logic models are described under Action Step 5 in "Take Action: Develop a Community Action Plan" in part II.)

✓ Survey coalition members and other decision makers to determine if your coalition is making the most of community resources to achieve its goals.

✓ Instead of counting numbers, explain an effort's return on investment (ROI), such as how it might save lives (Ralser 2007, 159).

✓ Use short-term results to make the case for or support how this strategy will have long-term benefits.

When should we evaluate? Evaluation is likely to be more positive and its results more useful if you build in evaluation early and make it an ongoing process. Plan evaluation before strategies begin to clarify program goals and reasonable outcomes. Use **TOOL 23: Are You Ready to Evaluate?** to help your coalition decide if it is prepared to begin evaluation activities (Mancini et al. 2004, 7-21; Patton 2008, 43-5).

Decide what type of evaluation you should conduct. Once you are ready and commit to evaluation, choose the type of evaluation that you wish to conduct. Evaluation can be characterized as being either formative or summative:

• **Formative evaluation** looks at the activities and outputs in your logic model or what makes an initiative work (the process). Often, we concentrate only on our strategic outcomes and miss opportunities to measure key changes and success that ultimately lead to our outcomes.

• **Summative evaluation** looks at the short-term, intermediate, and long-term outcomes that are identified in your logic model. Whatever design you choose, using both qualitative and quantitative methods is recommended.

TOOL 23: Are You Ready to Evaluate?	Yes	No
1. Are partners committed to evaluate and heed results?	❏	❏
2. Are coalition's goals realistic?	❏	❏
3. Are strategies consistent with coalition's goals?	❏	❏
4. Are desired results specific enough to be assessed?	❏	❏
5. Are strategies grounded in theory/prior evidence?	❏	❏
6. Do you know what kinds of data will be needed?	❏	❏
7. Are data available, and do you know how to access them?	❏	❏
8. Does anything limit/constrain access to these data?	❏	❏
9. Will results be used to make strategic decisions?	❏	❏
10. Will findings be used to assess whether strategies should extend to new populations/settings?	❏	❏
11. Are there evaluation resources that can be shared or obtained (funds, time, expertise, partner support)?	❏	❏
12. Will evaluation address key questions and be translated into "lessons learned"?	❏	❏

Moreover, evaluation can also be conducted by using *quantitative*, *qualitative* or *mixed* methods:

- **Quantitative methods** focus on counting and classifying the answers to your evaluation questions and constructing statistical models to explain what is observed.
- **Qualitative methods** provide detailed, and often narrative, answers to your evaluation questions and are used to explore a topic or confirm quantitative findings.

What Are the Steps for Conducting an Evaluation?

The following six steps will help tailor the evaluation of the strategies in your community action plan. The steps do not have to be done sequentially, but each should be addressed in a cyclical fashion (Centers for Disease Control and Prevention 1999).

Steps for Conducting Your Evaluation

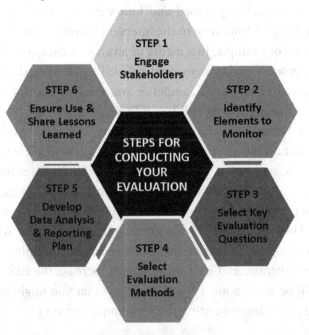

Step 1. Engage stakeholders. This step involves identifying and engaging stakeholders who have a vested interest in the evaluation. Find out what they want to know and how they will use the information. Involve them in identifying what sources of data currently exist in the community, as well as in helping to design and/or conduct the evaluation. Keep less-involved stakeholders informed about activities through meetings, reports, and other communications. Include internal and external partners as stakeholders. Internal partners are usually members of the coalition; external partners might be experts in social marketing, behavior change, communication, health promotion, and specific health issues. Keep in touch with stakeholders, and get input throughout the initiative and evaluation.

Step 2. Identify elements to monitor. In this step, you must decide what to monitor. Ask who will use the information and how, what resources are available, and whether data can be collected in a systematic, ethical manner. Monitoring (or process evaluation) is an ongoing effort that tracks factors such as funding received, products/services delivered, payments made, other contributed or expended resources, activities, and adherence to timelines. Monitoring lets you know whether strategies are being implemented as planned and how well they reach your priority audience(s). If problems arise in the intervention phase, make mid-course corrections. For example, in a media or awareness campaign for tobacco cessation, process evaluation would be used to monitor the campaign's reach, message effectiveness, audience awareness of your website or helpline, and changes in attitudes toward tobacco use.

Step 3. Select key evaluation questions. Before you begin to evaluate, you must decide what questions you want answered. These questions will drive the evaluation, not the other way around. Refer back to your logic model. Questions about each part of the model (inputs, activities, and outputs) will clarify how desired outcomes or changes might be reached. Then, clarify the evaluation's purpose and who will use the results to focus the evaluation questions and your communication plan. Evaluating with the end user in mind will increase the likelihood that results will be used. Some typical questions that you might want to ask about the group implementing the community action plan include:

- What resources have been most helpful or are needed?
- What are the associated costs of these resources?
- Do our strategies fit our partners' mission and goals?
- Are our strategies successful?
- Do our strategies reach intended groups?
- What have we accomplished?

Basic evaluation questions that focus on your strategies may include:

- What aspects of its strategies will be evaluated?
- Was fidelity to the action plan maintained?
- Were exposure levels to the strategies adequate to make a measurable difference?
- What level of performance must be reached for the strategy to be considered successful?
- What evidence will be used to indicate how the intervention has performed?

- How will the lessons learned from the evaluation be used to improve the community's health?

Step 4. Determine how information will be gathered. In this step, you and/or the team must decide how to gather data. The choice of design will determine what counts as evidence, how it will be gathered and processed, and what results can be inferred based on the evidence. Develop the right research design for your situation. Choices include:

- **Experimental designs.** Use random assignment to create intervention and control groups. Administer intervention to one group; then compare groups on a measure of interest to see if the intervention worked.
- **Quasi-experimental designs.** No random assignment of participants to groups occurs.
- **Cross-sectional designs.** This is a snapshot of participants or groups using observation, surveys, focus groups, and/or key informant interviews on certain measures via telephone, Internet, face-to-face interviews, and so forth.
- **Case study designs.** Each individual or situation is considered unique and investigated in depth.

Decide which existing information sources will be used and what methods will be used to gather information from new sources. The overall goal is to get useful information to key decision makers in a cost-effective, feasible way. Use a combination of methods—surveys to collect information quickly from many people, and interviews to get more in-depth information from key informants. Case studies provide in-depth analyses of those who benefited or not from the strategy. Consider these questions when deciding which methods to use:

- What information is needed to make decisions about a strategy or activity?
- How much can be collected and analyzed economically and practically?
- How accurate is the information?

- What methods should be used if more data is needed?
- Will information seem credible to decision makers (such as to funders or top management?)
- Will the community in question be willing to complete surveys, engage in interviews and focus groups, and allow document review?
- Who can use the methods now? Is training needed?

Review your short-term, intermediate, and long-term outcomes and measures and consider what data will be needed to help you assess those outcomes. Outcome measures identify expected effects or levels of success needed to meet your action plan and are based on expected changes from a known baseline.

Many sources of information can be used to gather data for about your coalition and its efforts, as shown in **TOOL 24: Sources of Information**.

TOOL 24: Sources of Information

Existing Data
- Coalition documents: reports, minutes, newsletters and rosters
- Existing databases
- Agency, media, school/business records or websites

People
- Coalition members
- Participants
- General public
- Key informants (funders, agency officials)

Other
- Actual events, activities and practices
- Before and after pictures
- Maps, charts

Various data collection methods can be used to collect information—most community researchers rely on the tried-and-true surveys or focus groups. Be bold and try using a combination of the other methods that are shown in **TOOL 25: A Dozen Data Collection Methods** (Taylor-

Powell, Rossing and Geran 1998). Your community may find them to be more engaging and less intimidating. For example, observing how many parents at a pre-school put an infant in a safety seat before driving home is easy and gives instant actionable information for your coalition's safety agenda. Likewise, having teens take photographs that illustrate what the term "healthy living" means for their neighborhood may be instructive for your prevention efforts.

TOOL 25: A Dozen Data Collection Methods	
Survey	Mailed, electronic, in-person or by phone
Case study	Detailed data collection using multiple sources and methods
Interviews	May be in-person, by phone, or through a focus group
Observation	Data collection via trained interviewers
Group assessment	Structured brainstorms or forums
Expert/peer review	Examination by peers or expert panels
Portfolio review	Samples of materials/work to assess scope and quality
Testimonials	Personal responses and reactions by key participants
Tests	Standard measures of knowledge and performance
Photographs/videos	Collection of visual images and stories
Diaries and journals	Chronological record of events that reveal personal views
Logs	Factual, brief chronological records
Document analysis	Content analysis to assess print materials

The purpose, advantages, and disadvantages of the most common data collection methods are shown in **TOOL 26: Methods for Collecting Evaluation Data**, while a sample evaluation plan is shown in **TOOL 27: Sample Evaluation Plan.**

TOOL 26: Methods for Collecting Evaluation Data			
Method	Purpose	Advantages	Challenges
Surveys, Checklists	Quickly and easily gather information	- Complete anonymously - Inexpensive - Easy to compare and analyze - Administer to many - Provides extensive data - Sample surveys exist	- Might not get careful feedback - Wording can bias responses - Are impersonal - May need sampling expert - Doesn't get full story
Interviews	Understand Participants' experiences or learn more about survey answers	- Get full range and depth of information - Builds relationship with participant - Flexible	- Time consuming - Hard to analyze and compare - Costly - Interviewer bias
Document Review	Get impression of how program operates—review minutes, and finances	- Provides deep historical data - Doesn't interrupt program routine - Information is available - Few biases	- Takes time - Incomplete info - Need clarity on what you want - Data restricted to what exists
Observation	Gather data about how program actually operates	- View strategies as they occur - Can adapt to events as they occur	- Hard to interpret behaviors and categorize observations - May influence behaviors - Expensive

TOOL 27: Sample Evaluation Plan									
		Data Collection					Design		
Key evaluation question(s)	Measures/ outcomes	Survey/scale	Interview	Self-report/log	Observation	Archival records	Case study	Pre-posttest Control Group	Time series
Planning and implementation ?s	**Process Descriptive/ Process Measures**								
Who participates?	Demographic data	X	X				X		
Why do participants drop out?	Reasons for drop out	X	X				X		
Are different activities generated?	Type and frequency of activities				X	X	X		
Goal attainment	**Process**								
How many involved?	# of participants			X	X	X	X		X
How many hours are participants involved?	# of hours by activity			X	X	X	X		X
How many people are trained?	# of participants per workshop			X	X	X	X		X
Participant impact Impact on Participants	**Short-term**								
Did attitudes/ behavior change?	Changes in attitude and behavior	X	X	X	X	X		X	X
Does participation affect incidence of problems?	Incidence of problems	X	X			X		X	
Are participants satisfied?	Participants' satisfaction ratings	X					X		
Community impact	**Intermediate and long-term**								
What resulted from intervention?	Changes in programs, policies and practices	X	X	X	X	X			X
Do strategic benefits outweigh costs?	Cost-benefit data		X	X		X	X		
Are community and participants satisfied with services?	Participant/ community satisfaction ratings	X					X		

Step 5. Develop a data analysis and reporting plan. Describe the research techniques used to analyze data and report findings, disseminate the report to partners and stakeholders, collect feedback, and use it to modify strategies. Consider the following questions:

- How will data for monitoring and evaluation questions be summarized and analyzed?
- How will conclusions be justified?
- How will stakeholders (inside and outside the coalition) stay informed about monitoring and evaluation activities?
- What is the timeline for monitoring and evaluating tasks? How will they coordinate with implementation activities?
- What is the budget for monitoring and evaluating, and how will it be presented? How will monitoring and evaluating data be reported?

Step 6. Ensure use and share lessons learned. Effective evaluation requires time, effort, and resources. Findings should be disseminated widely and used for informed decision making and action. Key stakeholders can provide critical information about how findings are disseminated to maximize their use. Consider the following questions:

- What feedback was received concerning the strategy?
- How can we use evaluation summary information to revise the strategy?
- How will this information impact our internal/external communication plans?
- What are the lessons learned?

This step is critical for your coalition leaders and members. It clarifies what the evaluation findings mean for your community. The plan helps you reflect on how your work has made a difference and how it can be improved. Use it as a time to celebrate successes and get ready for the future.

Expand or End Your Coalition When Goals Are Reached

Success is not final; failure in life is not fatal,
it is the courage to continue that counts.
—Sir Winston Churchill

After a funding opportunity has ended, a community coalition may continue on according to several different scenarios. The coalition may do the following:

- Function exactly as it did before—with the same vision, goals, membership, activities, structures, intensity of collaboration, and community buy-in.
- Develop a different composition of members, although the coalition still continues to address its original goals.
- Scale back its work by addressing one or two original goals.
- Expand to work toward new goals.
- Adopt new goals as a result of a shift in the social/political environment or changes in the community's needs.

Coalitions may not continue after initial funding ends. Some dissolve because of internal problems; others actively disband because they find new homes for their activities within the community (e.g., institutionalization of strategies or activities within the community) or because they have achieved their original goals.

Just as a campfire must be doused, you eventually may be faced with the decision of whether or not to disband your coalition. The critical issue here is that you make a decision. Many coalitions simply fade away—goals are not reformulated, funding is not obtained, recruitment ceases, and members vote with their feet to leave the coalition. This sets up a poor pattern for the community and leaves a legacy of failure for future collaborations. If you find most of the items in **TOOL 28: Should You Disband Your Coalition?** ring true, then you might consider disbanding the coalition to be your best option. It's better to reach closure with the coalition—celebrate what went well, thank the partner organizations and members for their work, and leave the community with hope for future endeavors.

TOOL 28: Should You Disband Your Coalition?

- ❑ Members applaud the coalition's past, but lack hope for its future.
- ❑ General atmosphere of conflict, discontent, and/or malaise exists.
- ❑ Little or no recruitment of new members occurs.
- ❑ Members rarely or inconsistently attend meetings and events.
- ❑ Member organizations do not participate in coalition activities.
- ❑ Leaders and members do not follow through on or share tasks.
- ❑ Members do not generate in-kind or financial resources for the coalition.
- ❑ Members do not volunteer to run for elected leadership positions.
- ❑ Communication among members, staff and members, and the coalition and community is fragmented or lacking.
- ❑ Members cannot recall what the coalition has accomplished.
- ❑ Strategic and action plans are not reviewed or renewed.
- ❑ The coalition is unknown or not connected to the broader community.

- • If fewer than six of these items are checked, try suggested solutions in **TOOL 21: What to Do When Things Go Wrong.**
- • If six or more of these items are checked, consider disbanding the coalition. It can always be rebuilt with renewed vision or purpose at a later time.

SUSTAIN YOUR COALITION

RECAP

- Given the scarcity of resources and greater competition for funding, your community needs to maintain its capacity to work in partnership on its priority issues, so that the strategies they put in place will have lasting, or sustainable, impact.
- A coalition needs a stable base of operations—a "community home" and/or fiscal agent to position its efforts in the community and ensure that essential functions continue, even in the face of internal and external change.
- For sustainability, coalitions need: involvement in significant community activities; strategic capacity; clear values or operating principles; core leadership with strong commitment, management capacity, community buy-in and support; and power and influence.
- The hallmarks of a fiscally sound non-profit organization are: diversity in funding sources; ability to generate funds internally; multi-year funding; and a sustainable structure, such as a community home and/or fiscal agent or 501 c 3 non-profit statuses.

Evaluation Resources

American Evaluation Association. This comprehensive website includes several handbooks and texts available online. Most documents focus on "how to's" of evaluation-related subjects. http://www.eval.org/Resources/onlinehbtxt.htm

Annie E. Casey Foundation. Reisman, J, Gienapp, A, & Stachowiak, S. (Authors). (2007). **A Guide for Evaluating Advocacy and Policy.** Baltimore, MD: AECF. This guide helps determine ways to measure and evaluate the impact of advocacy and public policy. It lays out a framework for naming outcomes associated with advocacy and policy work, as well as directions for evaluation design that include a broad range of methods, intensities, audiences, timeframes and purposes. http://www.aecf.org/upload/PublicationFiles/DA3622H5000.pdf

Annie E. Casey Foundation. **Kids Count On-line Data Book.** This website contains state-level data for over seventy-five measures of child well-being. This database helps generate custom profiles for a geographic area or to compare areas on a topic. http://www.aecf.org/kidscount/sld/

CDC CHANGE Tool. This tool helps stakeholders survey their community, offers examples of PSE change strategies, and provides feedback for making local-level change for healthy living. For each of the tool's sectors, questions are posed about demographics, physical activity, nutrition, tobacco, chronic disease management, and leadership. CHANGE helps coalition members *track progress* on a five-point scale. As problems are identified and health-related PSE change strategies are put in place, community-level changes can be tracked. http://www.cdc.gov/healthy-communitiesprogram/tools/change/pdf/changeactionguide.pdf

CDC Common Community Measures for Obesity Prevention. This resource recommends 24 strategies and measures that communities can use to plan and monitor PSE changes for obesity prevention. Strategies are sorted into 6 categories: 1) promote availability of affordable healthy food and beverages), 2) support healthy food and beverage choices, 3) encourage breastfeeding, 4) promote physical activity or limit sedentary activity among youth, 5) create safe communities that support physical activity, and 6) encourage communities to organize for change. http://www.cdc.gov/mmwr/preview/mmwrhtml/rr5807a1.htm

CDC Implementation and Measurement Guide. This was developed by the Division of Nutrition, Physical Activity, and Obesity to assist governments, states, and policy makers to implement obesity prevention strategies and report on associated measurements. It includes measurement data protocols, resources, and examples of communities that successfully implemented each strategy. http://www.cdc.gov/obesity/downloads/community_strategies_guide.pdf

CDC Framework for Program Evaluation in Public Health. Morbidity and Mortality Weekly Report, 48 (RR-11) The framework helps guide health professionals to evaluate programs and integrate evaluation into program activities. It summarizes the essential elements, steps, and standards of effective program evaluation.
http://www.cdc.gov/eval/framework/index.htm.

Community Anti-Drug Coalitions of America (CADCA). The Coalition Institute's Guiding Principles for Coalition Evaluation. Washington, DC: Author. This guide provides a general framework for designing an evaluation specific to coalitions and offers guiding principles to help coalitions plan an evaluation. http://www.coalitioninstitute.org/Evaluation-Research/Strategizer48.pdf

Community Toolbox. **Evaluating community programs and initiatives.** This web-based resource was created and is maintained by the University of Kansas. It provides user-friendly instructions for planning, implementing, and evaluating community health and development initiatives. The evaluation section includes step-by-step guidelines, examples, checklists of major points, and training materials for such efforts.
http://ctb.ukans.edu.

Collaborative Solutions. Tom Wolff & Associates provide tools and resources necessary to create collaborations, enhance healthy communities, and build community coalitions. Publications such as the twenty-eight *Coalition Building Tip Sheets* cover issues from start up to sustainability
http://www.tomwolff.com/

Drug Strategies. Assessing Community Coalitions. This manual, funded by the Robert Wood Johnson and Knight Foundations, provides a history of drug abuse prevention coalition efforts in the United States, as well as their evaluations, and explores elements that contributed to their effectives. Resources and survey instruments are available at http://www.drugstrategies.org/acrobat/CommCoal.pdf

Empowerment Evaluation Website: The Collaborative, Participatory, and Empowerment Evaluation group, of the American Evaluation Association, sponsors this site that includes survey software and self-help manuals. http://www.stanford.edu/~davidf/empowermentevaluation.html

Innovative Network (InnonNet). Helping Agencies Succeed. This web-based resource makes evaluation tools and resources available to nonprofits and funders across program type, organization size, and geographic boundaries. An interactive "workstation" leads users through steps to define program goals, identify activities to achieve them, design steps for evaluating activities and outcomes, and create a budget for conducting the project and evaluation. Users can submit their plans for comments by InnoNet staff. www.innonet.org.

Join Together. How Do We Know We are Making a Difference: A Community Alcohol, Tobacco and Drug Indicators Handbook. (2005). Boston, Massachusetts. This revised handbook has been used by community groups nationwide to evaluate activities focused on preventing and reducing harms from substance use. It is designed to direct you through the process of planning an indicator reporting program, selecting relevant indicators and measures, collecting local data, and reporting to your target audience. http://indicatorshandbook.org/indicators/

Kettel Khan, L, Sobush, K, Keener, D, Goodman, K, Lowry, A, Kakietek, J, Zaro, S., *Div. of Nutrition, Physical Activity & Obesity, National Center for Chronic Disease Prevention and Health Promotion, CDC, CDC Foundation, ICF Macro.* **Recommended Community Strategies and Measurements to Prevent Obesity in the United States.** *MMWR, 58/* RR07:1-26. This report describes the expert panel process that identified 6 categories and 24 recommended strategies for obesity prevention and suggested measurements for each strategy that communities can use to assess performance and track progress. www.cdc.gov/mmwr/preview/mmwrhtml/rr5807a1.htm

National Neighborhood Indicators Project. A collaborative effort by the Urban Institute and local partners to develop and use neighborhood information systems in local policy-making and community building. http://www.urban.org/nnip/

National Science Foundation. **The 2002 User-Friendly Handbook for Project Evaluation.** This handbook was developed for managers of NSF-funded education programs to increase their understanding of the evaluation process, as well as to build their capacity to communicate with evaluators and manage the actual evaluation. www.nsf.gov/pubs/2002/nsf02057/start.htm.

The following companies provide software for survey development:

- *SurveyKey* – http://www.surveykey.com/
- **Survey Monkey** - http://www.surveymonkey.com/
- **Survey Suite** – http://intercom.virginia.edu/cgi-bin/cgiwrap/intercom/SurveySuite/ss_index.pl
- *Formsite* - http://www.formsite.com
- *Zoomerang* – http://www.zoomerang.com

Thompson NJ, & McClintock, HO. *Demonstrating your Program's Worth: A Primer on Evaluation for Programs to Prevent Unintentional Injury.* (2000). Atlanta, GA: CDC, National Center for Injury Prevention and Control. This books shows community programs how to demonstrate the value of their work to the public, to their peers, to funding agencies, and to the people they serve. It details how to conduct simple evaluation, how to hire and supervise consultants for complex evaluation, and how to incorporate evaluation activities into the activities of injury prevention or other health promotion programs. http://www.cdc.gov/ncipc/pub-res/dypw/dypw.pdf

United Way of America. **Measuring Program Outcomes.** This guide helps directors and program managers in human services measure outcomes for direct services, as well as advocacy, public education, capacity building, and other related efforts. It leads users through steps for measuring outcomes, from getting ready to do it to using findings. http://www.odesinc.org/Measuring_Program_Outcomes-UW.pdf

University of Wisconsin-Cooperative Extension. **Evaluating Collabora-tives.** Individuals who evaluate the work of coalitions and collaborations will find ideas and research to choose from to increase their effectiveness. http://learningstore.uwex.edu/Assets/pdfs/G3658-08.pdf

W.K. Kellogg Foundation. The **Evaluation Handbook** was developed for project directors as a framework for considering evaluation as a tool for program improvement. It provides information for planning and evaluating with or without assistance from an external evaluator. http://www.wkkf.org/Pubs/Tools/Evaluation/Pub770.pdf

Other Sustainability Resources

The Sustainability Planning Guide for Healthy Communities, by M. Batan, F. D. Butterfoss, A. Jaffe, and T. LaPier, uses science- and practice-based evidence to help coalitions, public health professionals, and community stakeholders create, implement, and evaluate their sustainability plans. It suggests a process for sustaining policy strategies and related activities, introduces varied approaches to sustainability, and demonstrates sustainability planning in action with examples. (CDC Division of Adult and Community Health, Healthy Communities Program, Atlanta, Georgia. 2011). http://www.cdc.gov/healthycommunitiesprogram/pdf/sustainability_guide.pdf

Center for Civic Partnerships. **Sustainability Toolkit: 10 Steps to Maintaining Your Community Improvements, 2nd Ed.** This toolkit shows how to create a community sustainability plan. (Sacramento, California: Public Health Institute.) http://www.civicpartnerships.org/docs/publications/sustainability_toolkit.htm.

Center for Public Health Systems Science (CPHSS), George Warren Brown School of Social Work, Washington University, St. Louis, Missouri. **Program Sustainability Assessment Tool.** This forty-item self-assessment can be used by stakeholders and staff members to rate their public health, social service or clinical care program/coalition/set of activities across eight sustainability components. After completing the tool online, an automated summary report of overall sustainability is generated that can be used for sustainability planning. https://sustaintool.org

Community Antidrug Coalitions of America (CADCA). **Sustainability Primer: Fostering Long-Term Change to Create Drug-Free Communities.** This primer offers a basic understanding of sustainability and its value in reducing long-term rates of substance abuse. It will help you identify what strategies your community should continue and the resources needed to create an effective sustainability plan. http://www.cadca.org/resources/detail/sustainability-primer

Ontario Healthy Communities Coalition. **From the Ground Up: An Organizing Handbook for Healthy Communities.** Toronto, Ontario, Canada: The Search Institute. This workbook provides a starting point for organizing healthy communities' efforts. http://www.ohcc-ccso.ca/en/from-the-ground-up-an-organizing-handbook-for-healthy-communities.

University of Kansas. **Community Toolbox**. Lawrence, KS. Chapters 42-44 focus on preparing an annual budget, accounting, contracting for service, and starting a community micro-grants program. Chapters 45-46 cover how to conduct a social marketing effort and plan for long-term sustainability of the effort. http://ctb.ukans.edu.

Wolff, T. (2010). **Tools for Sustainability.** Global Journal for Community Psychology Practice. 1(1):40-57. This publication highlights a sustainability planning process for non-profit organizations that involves four steps: 1. Who are you now as a coalition? 2. Where do you want to get to? Develop a shared understanding of sustainability. 3. What do you want to sustain? Assess what you are doing now. 4) How are we getting there? It includes worksheets and other valuable references. http://www.gicpp.org

AFTERWORD

Building coalitions and partnerships is not easy. Challenges arise every day when you combine the ideas, talents, and resources of diverse community sectors, coalitions, organizations, and individuals to reach effective actions. Coalition coordinators and leaders must develop skills in facilitation, communication, negotiation, management, and leadership, as well as issue-specific and technical knowledge in order to build and sustain effective coalitions. Again, I urge students and community professionals who seek a more comprehensive, academic foundation for working with coalitions to turn to *Coalitions and Partnerships in Community Health* (Butterfoss 2007) as a reference text.

Ignite is a field guide for community practitioners and community builders at every level. You are the ones who are charged to keep the flame of hope and optimism alive when community agencies, organizations, and individuals are discouraged or have lost their way. A coalition approach demands a clear vision and mission that light the way toward community action. It demands an infrastructure that is strong, yet flexible and responsive to changes that occur in the community and surrounding environment. It requires a diverse and innovative set of partners who are planners and doers and are willing to step out of their comfort zones to try promising, new approaches to solve critical community problems. It depends on developing a rich portfolio of financial and in-kind resources to support its efforts. Finally, it rests on the commitment and resolve of the community as a whole to believe that change is possible and to do the work required to make change happen.

Our communities basically want the same things—safe, clean environments; affordable, adequate housing and transportation; educational opportunities; accessible, quality health care; meaningful work at a fair wage; and equitable services for everyone. So, in the spirit of warmth and energy that our campfire metaphor brings, I invite each of you to be the spark that ignites your community to be safer, healthier, and fairer—and *fired up* for change.

GLOSSARY OF TERMS

Action plan—A written plan that outlines a community's goals, and the strategies, action steps, time line and responsible agents for reaching those goals.

Advocate—A change agent; one who supports or promotes a cause or defends the interests of others.

Community assessment—The measurement of a community's assets and needs to determine the best course of action to improve its quality of life.

Capacity—A coalition's ability to achieve its mission effectively and sustain itself by relying on its members' skills and capabilities.

Capacity building—The process of improving an organization or coalition's ability to achieve its mission by increasing skills and knowledge; ability to plan and implement programs, practices, and policies; quality, quantity, or cost-effectiveness of its work; and sustainability of its infrastructure and support systems.

Coalition—A group of diverse organizations/constituencies working together toward a common goal.

Collaboration—A working relationship among organizations that involves shared resources, rewards, responsibility, and risks, as well as accountability for success.

Collective impact—The commitment of groups from different sectors to solve a complex social problem that requires a backbone organization, a common agenda, shared measurement, mutually reinforcing activities, and continuous communication.

Commitment letter—A non-binding, written agreement that is used to clarify members' roles, organizational intentions, and levels of support and commitment to the coalition.

Community assets—The community's organizations, facilities, people, partnerships, regulations, policies, funding, and positive collective experience.

Community context—Community characteristics that may enhance or inhibit coalition function and influence how it develops, such as geography, demographics, politics, trust, and readiness.

Community needs—The negative physical, psychological, social, and environmental conditions found in communities.

Community planning—Assessment of a community's needs and the capacities or assets that can be mobilized to meet those needs.

Diversity—The inclusion of different types of people or community sectors in a coalition or organization.

Evaluation—A systematic assessment of the significance and merit of an initiative or program using standard criteria and measurement. It determines the value or level of achievement of goals, enables reflection, and identifies areas for improvement.

Goal—A desired result that an organization or coalition envisions, plans, and commits to achieve.

Healthy communities—Communities help people make healthy choices where they live, learn, work, pray, and play through sustainable changes focusing on tobacco use, physical inactivity, and unhealthy eating.

Coalition infrastructure—The basic physical and organizational structures that support a coalition and its work, such as governance, resources, leaders, members, and procedures.

Lead agency—The convening agency that provides managerial support and/or fiscal oversight for a coalition; community home.

Logic model—A graphical depiction of the relationships between a program or initiative's resources or inputs, activities, outputs, and outcomes.

Memorandum of understanding (MOU)—A document that describes a mutual agreement between two or more organizations, such as a coalition and its partners.

Mission statement—A written declaration of an organization's or coalition's core purpose and focus of work.

MOU—Memorandum of understanding.

Non-profit organization—An incorporated organization or coalition that exists for charitable or educational reasons. Money earned must be retained by the coalition and used for its expenses, operations, and programs.

Objectives—Incremental benchmarks that aid in reaching the goals of an organization or coalition.

Outcomes—The short-term, intermediate, and long-term results of an organization's or coalition's work

Organizational message—A 1-page document that communicates the coalition's unique purpose, scope of activities, and priority population. It is used for media coverage, to recruit community members, and to introduce the coalition to potential partners or funders.

Partnership—A collaborative arrangement between at least two organizations to reach mutual goals.

Policies, systems, and environment (PSE) change—Modifying the environment to make healthy choices practical and available to all community members, by changing laws, rules, and shaping physical landscapes that impact behavior.

Priority setting—A process of helping coalitions to make logical decisions. It involves considering mission, vision, and values; available resources; local conditions; what other organizations are doing; and research on best and promising practices.

PSE—Policies, systems, and environments.

Steering committee—The coalition's leadership body that includes chairs and vice-chairs of the coalition and its work groups, at-large members, and staff members. An executive committee of officers may be a subgroup of the steering committee.

Sustainability—A coalition's ongoing capacity and resolve to work together to establish, advance, and maintain effective strategies that continuously improve health and quality of life for all.

SWOT analysis—A review of a coalition's *strengths* and *weaknesses*, as well as *opportunities* and *threats* that exist in the broader environment. This process identifies strategic issues to be addressed and sets priorities in terms of importance or time.

Technical assistance—Tailored guidance to meet specific needs of a coalition or organization through collaborative communication with a trainer or specialist; takes into account culture and circumstances and can be provided in person or via phone, mail, e-mail, or Internet.

Transformational leadership—A type of leadership used by coalitions whereby leaders are able to inspire others to accomplish great things and inextricably link them in transformative change; servant leadership.

Value statements—The organization or coalition's core principles that focus on equity and how culture affects health and quality of life; used to craft mission statements.

Vision—An aspirational description of what a coalition or organization would like to achieve and guides them in choosing current and future actions.

Work group—A subgroup of the coalition that focuses on a specific goal or set of goals.

REFERENCES

Part I: Before You Build It

Butterfoss, F.D. 2007. *Coalitions and Partnerships in Community Health*. San Francisco: JosseyBass.

Butterfoss, F.D., R. Goodman, and A. Wandersman. 1993. Community coalitions for prevention and health promotion. *Health Education Research* 8(3), 315-30.

Butterfoss, F.D., and M. C. Kegler. 2009. Toward a Comprehensive Understanding of Community Coalitions: Moving from Practice to Theory, 2nd Ed. In *Emerging Theories in Health Promotion Practice and Research*, ed. R. DiClemente, R. Crosby, and M. C. Kegler, 237-76, San Francisco: JosseyBass.

Chavis, D., and P. Florin. 1990. *Community Development, Community Participation and Substance Abuse Prevention*. San Jose: Prevention Office, Bureau of Drug Abuse Services.

Clark, N., L. J. Doctor, A. R. Friedman, L. L. Lachance, C. R. Houle, X. Geng, and J. A. Grisso. 2006. *Community* Coalitions to Control Chronic Disease: Allies Against Asthma as a Model and Case Study. *Health Promotion Practice* 7(2) suppl: 14-22S.

Cohen, L., V. Chavez, and S. Chemini. *2010. Prevention is Primary: Strategies for Community Well Being*. San Francisco: Jossey Bass.

Feighery, E., and T. Rogers. 1989. *Building and Maintaining Effective Coalitions*. Palo Alto: Health Promotion Resource Center, Stanford Center for Research in Disease Prevention.

Gray, B. 1996. Cross-sectoral partners: Collaborative alliances among business, government and communities. In C. Huxham, ed., *Creating Collaborative Advantage*. London: Sage Publications.

Kania, J., and M. Kramer. 2011. Collective impact. *Stanford Social Innovation Review* Winter: 36-41.

Mattesich, P., M. Murray-Close, and B. Monsey. 2001. *Collaboration: What Makes it Work—A Review of the Research Literature on Factors Influencing Successful Collaboration,* 2nd Ed. St. Paul: Amherst H. Wilder Foundation.

Ontario Healthy Communities Coalition. (2002). In *From the Ground Up: An Organizing Handbook for Healthy Communities.* Toronto: The Search Institute. http://www.ohcc-ccso.ca/en/from-the-ground-up-an-organizing-handbook-for-healthy-communities.

Sofaer, S. 2001. *Working Together, Moving Ahead.* New York: City University of New York.

Whitt, M. 1993. *Fighting Tobacco: A Coalition Approach to Improving Your Community's Health.* Lansing: Michigan Department of Public Health.

Winer, M., and K. Ray. 1994. *Collaboration Handbook: Creating, Sustaining, and Enjoying the Journey.* St. Paul: Amherst H. Wilder Foundation.

Part II: Build It

Andringa, R., and T. Engstrom. 2001. *Nonprofit Board Answer Book: Practical Guidelines for Board Members and Chief Executives Size of the Board.* Washington: BoardSource.

Bass, B. M. 1985. *Leadership and Performance Beyond Expectations.* New York: The Free Press.

Bazzoli, G. J., E. Casey, J. A. Alexander, D. A. Conrad, S. A. Shortell, S. Sofaer, R. Hasnain-Wynia, and A. P. Zukoski. 2003. Collaborative initiatives: Where the rubber meets the road in community partnerships. *Medical Care Research and Review* 60(4), 63S-94S.

Bernhardt, J. M., J. D. Chaney, B. H. Chaney, and A. K. Hall. 2013. New media for health education: A revolution in progress. *Health Education & Behavior* 40(2): 129-32.

Bobowick, M.J., S. R. Hughes, and B. M. Lakey. 2001. *Transforming Board Structure.* Washington: BoardSource.

Burns, J. M. 1978. *Leadership.* New York: Harper & Row.

Butterfoss, F. D. 2007. *Coalitions and Partnerships in Community Health.* San Francisco: JosseyBass.

Butterfoss, F.D., and M. C. Kegler. 2009. Toward a Comprehensive Understanding of Community Coalitions: Moving from Practice to Theory, 2nd Ed. In *Emerging Theories in Health Promotion Practice and Research,* eds. R. DiClemente, R. Crosby, and M. C, Kegler, eds., 237-76. San Francisco: JosseyBass.

Campbell, A., M. Divine, and D. Young. 1990. *A Sense of Mission.* London: Economist Books.

Chrislip, D., and C. Larson. 1994. *Collaborative Leadership.* San Francisco: Jossey-Bass.

Clinical and Translational Science Awards (CTSA) Consortium's Community Engagement Key Function Committee. 2011. *Principles of Community Engagement, 2nd Ed.* Washington, DC: NIH Publication No. 11-7782. http://www.atsdr.cdc.gov/communityengagement/pdf/PCE_Report_508_FINAL.pdf

Coalitions Work. 2012. *Coalition Roles and Job Descriptions.* Yorktown: Coalitions Work. http://coalitionswork.com/wp-content/uploads/coalition_roles_and_job_descriptions.pdf).

Dambach, C. F., M. Davis, and R. L. Gale. 2009. *Structures and Practices of Nonprofit Boards,* 2nd Ed. Washington: BoardSource.

Dourado, P. 2007. *The 60 Second Leader: Everything You Need to Know About Leadership, in 60 Second Bites.* Chichester: Capstone Publishing Ltd.

Foster-Fishman, P., S. Berkowitz, D. Lounsbury, S. Jacobson, and N. Allen. 2001. Building collaborative capacity in community coalitions: A review and integrative framework. *American Journal of Community Psychology* 29(2):241-61.

Garza, H. 2005. Evaluating partnerships: Seven success factors. *The Evaluation Exchange,* 10(1):18-19. Boston: Harvard Family Research Project.

Heimlich, J. E., and S. H. Dresbach. 2004. Written Documents for Community Groups: Bylaws and Standard Operating Procedures. Fact Sheet on Community Development. Columbus: Ohio University. http://ohioline.osu.edu/cd-fact/co-bl.html

Himmelman, A. 2002. *Collaboration for a Change.* Minneapolis, MA: Himmelman Consulting.

Kaye, G. 2001. Grassroots involvement. *American Journal of Community Psychology* 29(2): 269-75.

Lasker, R. D., E. S. Weiss, and R. Miller. 2001. Partnership synergy: a practical framework for studying and strengthening the collaborative advantage. *Millbank Quarterly* 79(2):179-205.

Lolly, E. 2005. Working with diverse cultures. Ohio State University Extension Fact Sheet CDFS-14. Columbus: Author. http://ohioline.osu.edu/bc-fact/0014.html

Minkler, M. 2005. *Community Organizing and Community Building for Health and Welfare*, 3rd ed. New Brunswick: Rutgers University Press.

Mind Tools. Running Effective Meetings: Establishing an Objective and Sticking to It. http://www.mindtools.com/CommSkll/Running Meetings.htm

Nelson, R. B., and P. Economy. 1995. *Better Business Meetings*. Burr Ridge: Irwin Inc.

Nicola, B. Collaborative Leadership & Public Health - Developing a Culture of Shared Meaning. 2013. Seattle: University of Washington School of Public Health, Northwest Center for Public Health Practice. http://www.nwcphp.org/communications/publications/blogs/take-the-lead/collaborative-leadership-and-public-health

Northouse, P. G. 2013. *Leadership: Theory and Practice*, 6th Edition. Thousand Oaks: Sage.

Ohio Literary Resource Center. Transformative Leadership. http://literacy.kent.edu/Oasis/Leadership/over2.htm

Ralser, T. 2007. *ROI for Nonprofits: The New Key to Sustainability*. Hoboken: John Wiley & Sons.

Rosenthal, B. 1995. In G. Kaye and T. Wolff. The Inclusivity Checklist. *From the Ground Up: A Workbook on Coalition Building and Community Development*. Amherst: AHEC/Community Partners.

Roussos, S. T., and S. B. Fawcett. 2000. A review of collaborative partnerships as a strategy for improving community health. *Annual Review of Public Health* 21:369-402.

Rules Online. *Roberts Rules of Order.* http://www.rulesonline.com/rror-10.htm

Walker, V., and E. Heard. 2011. Board Governance. In D. R. Heyman, ed., *Nonprofit Management 101: A Complete and Practical Guide for Leaders and Professionals, 501-18.* San Francisco: Jossey Bass.

Wolff, T. 2001. Community coalition building—Contemporary practice and research. *American Journal of Community Psychology* 29(2):165-72.

Part III: Make It Work

Bartunek, J. M., P. G. Foster-Fishman, C. B. Christopher. 1996. Using Collaborative Advocacy to Foster Intergroup Cooperation: A Joint Insider-Outsider Investigation. *Human Relations* 49(6): 701-33.

Batan, M., F. D. Butterfoss, C. Jaffe, T. LaPier. 2011. *The Sustainability Planning Guide for Healthy Communities.* Atlanta: CDC Division of Adult and Community Health, Healthy Communities Program. http://www.cdc.gov/healthycommunitiesprogram/pdf/sustainability_guide.pdf

Bobo, K., J. Kendall, and S. Max. 2001. *Organizing for Social Change: Midwest Academy Manual for Activists.* Santa Ana: Seven Locks Press.

Bruner, C. 2004. Rethinking the evaluation of family strengthening strategies: Beyond traditional program evaluation models. *The Evaluation Exchange* 10(2): 1-5.

Butterfoss, F. D. 2007. *Coalitions and Partnerships in Community Health.* San Francisco: JosseyBass.

Butterfoss, F.D., and M. C. Kegler. 2009. Toward a Comprehensive Understanding of Community Coalitions: Moving from Practice to Theory, 2nd Ed. In *Emerging Theories in Health Promotion Practice and Research*, eds. R. DiClemente, R. Crosby, and M. C, Kegler, eds., *237-76.* San Francisco: JosseyBass.

Community Anti-Drug Coalitions Institute. 2009. The Coalition Impact: Environmental Prevention Strategies. Beyond the Basics: Topic-Specific Publications for Coalitions. Washington, DC: Community Anti-Drug Coalitions of America (CADCA). http://www.cadca.org/files/resources/Beyond_the-Basics-Environmental_Strategies-11-2010.pdf

Community Tool Box. Developing a Plan for Identifying Local Needs and Resources. Community Tool Box. Lawrence, KS: KU Work

Group for Community Health and Development. http://ctb.ku.edu/
en/tablecontents/sub_section_main_1019.aspx

County Health Rankings & Roadmaps. *Roadmaps to Health*.
University of Wisconsin Population Health Institute. http://www.
countyhealthrankings.org/roadmaps

Fixsen, D. L., Blasé, R.M., S. F. Naoom, K. and Wallace, F. 2009. Core
Implementation Components. *Research on Social Work Practice* 19:531-
40.

Foster-Fishman, P., S. Berkowitz, D. Lounsbury, S. Jacobson, and N. Allen.
2001. Building collaborative capacity in community coalitions: A
review and integrative framework. *American Journal of Community
Psychology* 29(2):241-61.

Frieden, T. R. 2010. A Framework for Public Health Action: The Health
Impact Pyramid. *American Journal of Public Health* 100(4):590-5.

McKenzie, J. F., B. L. Neiger, and R. Thackeray. 2008. *Planning, Implementing & Evaluating Health Promotion Programs*, 5th Ed., San Francisco:
Pearson/Benjamin Cummings.

National Resource Center. 2010. Conducting a Community
Assessment. *Strengthening Nonprofits: A Capacity Builder's Resource
Library*. Washington, DC: US Dept. of Health and Human
Services. http://strengtheningnonprofits.org/resources/guidebooks/
Community_Assessment.pdf

Rogers, E. M. 1995. *Diffusion of Innovations*. New York: Free Press.

Rosenthal, B. 1995. In *From the Ground Up: A Workbook on Coalition
Building & Community Development*. eds. Gillian Kaye & Thomas
Wolff, 59. Amherst: AHEC/Community Partners.

Schorr, L. 1997. *Common Purpose: Strengthening Families and Neighborhoods
to Rebuild America*. New York: Anchor Books Doubleday.

Wolf, T. 2012. *Managing a Nonprofit Organization: Updated Twenty-First-
Century Edition*. New York: Free Press.

Wolff, T. 2012. *The Power of Collaborative Solutions: Six Principles and Effective
Tools for Building Healthy Communities*. San Francisco: Jossey-Bass.

Part IV: Sustain It

Batan, M., F. D. Butterfoss, C. Jaffe, T. LaPier. 2011. *The Sustainability Planning Guide for Healthy Communities*. Atlanta: CDC Division of Adult and Community Health, Healthy Communities Program. http://www.cdc.gov/healthycommunitiesprogram/pdf/sustainability_guide.pdf

Bernhardt, J. M., D. Mays, and A. K. Hall. 2012. Social marketing at the right place and right time with new media. *Journal of Social Marketing* 2(2):130- 7.

Center for Civic Partnerships. 2010. *Sustainability Toolkit: 10 Steps to Maintaining Your Community Improvements, 2nd Ed.* Sacramento: Public Health Institute. http://www.civicpartnerships.org/docs/publications/sustainability_toolkit.htm.

Centers for Disease Control and Prevention. 1999. Framework for Program Evaluation in Public Health. *Morbidity and Mortality Weekly Report* 48(RR11) 1-40.

Community Tool Box. 2003. Developing a plan for financial sustainability. University of Kansas. http://ctb.ku.edu/en/tablecontents/sub_section_main_1297.aspx/

Lasker, R. D., and E. S. Weiss. 2003. Broadening participation in community problem solving: A multidisciplinary model to support collaborative practice and research. *Journal of Urban Health* 80(1), 14-48.

Leviton, L. C., C. Herrera, S. K. Pepper, N. Fishman, and D. P. Racine. 2006. Faith in Action: Capacity and sustainability of volunteer organizations. *Evaluation and Program Planning* 29(2): 201–7.

Mancini, J. A., L. I. Marek, R. A. Byrne, and A. J. Huebner. 2004. Community-Based Program Research: Context, Program Readiness and Evaluation Usefulness. *Journal of Community Practice* 12(1/2: 7-21).

Marek, L. I., J. A. Mancini, and D. J. Brock. 2009. Continuity, success, and survival of community-based projects: The National Youth at Risk Program Sustainability Study. Blacksburg: Virginia Cooperative Extension. http://pubs.ext.vt.edu/350/350-801/350-801.pdf

Mosaica: The Center for Nonprofit Development and Pluralism. 2005. *Sustainability*. Washington, DC: Author.

Patton, M. Q. 2008. *Utilization-Focused Evaluation*. Los Angeles: Sage.

Ralser, R. 2007. *ROI for Nonprofits: The New Key to Sustainability*. San Francisco: Wiley Press.

Silver, A. 2012. *How to Win Grants: 101 Winning Strategies*. New York: Allworth Press.

Taylor-Powell, E., B. Rossing, and J. Geran. 2010. *Evaluating Collaboratives: Reaching the Potential*. Madison: University of Wisconsin Cooperative Extension.

The NonProfit Times. 2012. 10 Vital *Nonprofit Marketing Techniques*. Morris Plains: Non Profit Times. http://www.thenonprofittimes.com/article/detail/10-vital-nonprofit-marketing-techniques-4564

Wolf, T. 2012. *Managing a Nonprofit Organization in the Twenty-First Century*. New York: Fireside/Simon & Schuster, Inc.

INDEX

152

Frances Dunn Butterfoss, PhD, MSEd, is a nation-
ally recognized expert on coalition building and organizational development, with more than twenty-
five years of experience training and consulting with
organizations, coalitions, and communities across
North America. She is president of Coalitions Work
and a professor at Eastern Virginia Medical School.
She has founded and directed several coalitions
and received research support from many agencies

and foundations. She has published widely, and her textbook, *Coalitions
and Partnerships in Community Health*, is a best seller for academics and
practitioners alike. Fran is a past president and distinguished fellow
of the Society for Public Health Education. She lives in Virginia with
her husband, Tom, and is devoted to their three children and four
grandchildren.

Printed in the United States
By Bookmasters